A
Trails Guide
Arizona
Phoenix Region

By CHARLES A. WELLS and MATT PETERSON

Go to
www.funtreks.com

Author Chuck Wells rides along south end of Bartlett Lake, Trail #18, difficult.

Easy • Moderate • Difficult
ATV Riding Adventures

FunTreks
Adventure
Responsibly

1

Published by FunTreks, Inc.
P. O. Box 3127, Monument, CO 80132-3127
Phone: Toll Free 877-222-7623, Fax: 719-277-7411
E-mail: books@funtreks.com, Web site: www.funtreks.com

Copyright © 2008 by FunTreks, Inc.

Edited by Shelley Mayer. Cover design, photography, maps, and production by
Charles A. Wells and Matt Peterson.

First Edition

Library of Congress Control Number 2008940019
ISBN 978-1-934838-02-0

Printed in China.

To order additional books, call toll-free 1-877-222-7623 or use order form in back of
this book. You may also order online at www.funtreks.com.

TRAIL UPDATES:
For latest trail updates and changes, check the *Trail Updates* page on our Web site at
www.funtreks.com.

GUARANTEE OF SATISFACTION:
If you are dissatisfied with this book in any way, regardless of where you bought it,
please call our toll-free number during business hours at 1-877-222-7623. We promise
to do whatever it takes to make you happy.

DISCLAIMER

Travel in Arizona's backcountry is, by its very nature, potentially dangerous and could result in property damage, injury, or even death. The scope
of this book cannot predict every possible hazard you may encounter. If you
ride any of the trails in this book, you acknowledge these risks and assume
full responsibility. You are the final judge as to whether a trail is safe to ride
on any given day, whether your vehicle is capable of the journey and what
supplies you should carry. The information contained herein cannot replace
good judgment and proper preparation on your part. The publisher and
author of this book disclaim any and all liability for bodily injury, death, or
property damage that could occur to you or any fellow travelers.

At the time this book was written, all routes were legal for OHV use.
However, new forest plans or other local changes could change route designation in the future. It is your responsibility to be aware of these changes
when or if they occur. (See page 17 for more details.)

ACKNOWLEDGMENTS

Our sincere thanks to the following individuals and organizations who helped with this book:

The U.S. Forest Service, Bureau of Land Management, Arizona Game and Fish Department, Arizona State Land Department, Agua Fria National Monument and Lake Pleasant Regional Park. We worked with a long list of hard-working staffers who provided courteous and professional advice.

Jim Ruhl, resident of Black Canyon City and avid ATV enthusiast. We met Jim at the Cleator Bar one weekend. Jim told us how he and his friends ride almost everywhere on their street registered ATVs on a broad network of dirt roads in the area. He invited us to join him on an exciting trail near his home, which appears in this book as Black Canyon, Trail #12.

Mike Knoles, owner of Arizona Hummer Tours. We ran into Mike on the trail while he was doing a Hummer tour of historic Gillette. Shortly thereafter, we got together with Mike and his friend John Flickinger, and they gave us a complete ATV tour of the area, including the old mining town of Tip Top and an interesting Indian fort. The end result was the Gillette Historic Tour, Trail #13.

Ryan Gibson, long-time Arizona Jeeper and creator of Arizona-Trailways.com. Ryan took a day off to lead us on Trail #11. Locals have several different names for this trail, but we decided to call it "Dead Cow Gulch." Although only a portion of the trail, "Dead Cow Gulch" was indicated on the Prescott National Forest map.

Jason DeMonto, an active member of Arizona's 5,000-member virtualjeepclub.com. Jason told us about a trail called "Log Corral" that he thought might be doable on an ATV, although he warned us it was difficult. We gave it a try and had the time of our lives. The route is described in this book as Log Corral to Bartlett Lake, Trail #18.

Tammy and Alan Czech, Jeepers we met near Butcher Jones Recreation area. They guided us to the first cove at Saguaro Lake, Trail #22.

Shelley Mayer, for her continued support as editor for FunTreks books. Shelley works for us on a project basis and has edited every book, except one, for all ten years we've been in business. We congratulate her on her recent retirement from her regular fulltime job, and look forward to continuing to work with her in the future.

Jaime Rae, business and finance, Darlene Teran, order fullfillment, and daughter, Marcia LeVault, sales and special projects. All have worked hard this last year and contributed to FunTreks' success. I'd also like to thank my wife, Beverly, for her continued support.

Finally, a special thanks to Matt Peterson, co-author of this book. Relatively new to FunTreks, Matt is learning what it takes to produce a good guidebook. Matt and I rode all the trails together and he wrote and produced a portion of the finished result.

Charles A. Wells

Maneuvering through narrow Box Canyon, Trail #26, Moderate.

CONTENTS

Page Topic

6   Trail List, Author's Favorites
7   Trail Locator Map
8   Trails Listed by Difficulty
9   Trail Ratings Defined

11 INTRODUCTION

12   The Benefits of Using This Book
13   How to Use This Book
14   The Right Trail for You
14   Arizona OHV Title and Registration Requirements
17   New Forest Plans
18   Safety Tips
20   Phoenix Weather Statistics
20   Trip Preparation
21   Checklist of Equipment and Supplies
22   Your Responsibilities as a Backcountry Rider
25   Courtesy and Ethics
26   Recommended Maps
27   Global Positioning (& GPS Settings)
28   Desert Survival
29   Final Comments
30   Map Legend

31 THE TRAILS

See next page for a complete listing of all trails and a locator map. Trail descriptions begin on page 31.

153 APPENDIX

154   References/Reading
155   Contact Information
158   About the Authors
159   Order Form for Other FunTreks Books
160   FunTreks Complete Line of Books

Trail List

UTVs: See notes at bottom of page.

No.	Trail	Page	Rating	UTVs
1.	Harquahala Mountain*	32	Easy	OK
2.	Belmont Mountain	36	Mod.	OK
3.	Vulture Mountain, Hassayampa River	40	Mod.	OK
4.	Wickenburg Mountains*	44	Mod.	OK
5.	Boulders OHV Area, Lower Loop	48	Easy	OK
6.	Boulders OHV Area, Upper Loop*	52	Diff.	Read
7.	Backway to Crown King*	56	Diff.	Read
8.	Tule Creek Homestead	60	Mod.	OK
9.	Northshore Lake Pleasant*	64	Easy	OK
10.	Desoto Mine	68	Diff.	Read
11.	Dead Cow Gulch	72	Mod.	OK
12.	Black Canyon	76	Mod.	OK
13.	Gillette Historic Tour	80	Easy	OK
14.	New River Canyon	84	Mod.	OK
15.	Desert Wells Multiuse Area	88	Easy	OK
16.	Bloody Basin, Sheep Bridge*	92	Easy	OK
17.	Sunflower Mine	96	Diff.	Read
18.	Log Corral to Bartlett Lake*	100	Diff.	Read
19.	Sycamore Creek, Sugarloaf Mtn.	104	Mod.	OK
20.	Rolls OHV Area, North	108	Easy	OK
21.	Rolls OHV Area, South*	112	Diff.	OK
22.	Saguaro Lake Coves	116	Diff.	OK
23.	Four Peaks*	120	Easy	OK
24.	Bulldog Canyon	124	Mod.	OK
25.	Montana Mountain*	128	Mod.	OK
26.	Box Canyon*	132	Mod.	OK
27.	Woodpecker, Ajax Loop	136	Diff.	Read
28.	Martinez Canyon*	140	Diff.	Read
29.	Coke Ovens	144	Diff.	OK
30.	Walnut Canyon*	148	Mod.	OK

*Author's Favorites

UTV refers to 60″-wide side-by-sides. "OK" means entire trail is suitable for UTVs. "Read" means READ TRAIL DESCRIPTION to find out which part of the trail may be too narrow or too difficult. "Rating" applies to ATVs. UTVs may find the trail more difficult.

Trail Locator Map

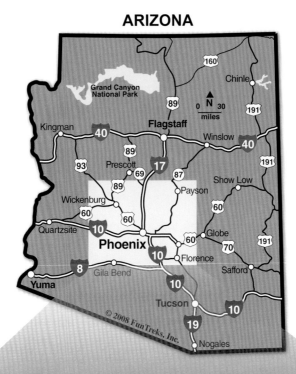

ARIZONA

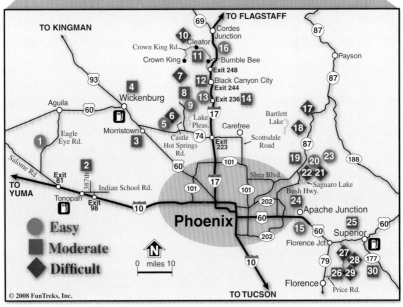

Trails Listed by Difficulty

Although trails are grouped into three major categories, there are still differences in difficulty within each group. For example, Trail #9 is easier than Trail #13, even though both are rated easy. Trails are progressively more difficult as you pan down the list, although you may have to skip several trails to see any significant difference.

No.	Trail	Page	Rating
15.	Desert Wells Multiuse Area	88	Easy
9.	Northshore Lake Pleasant	64	Easy
20.	Rolls OHV Area, North	108	Easy
23.	Four Peaks	120	Easy
1.	Harquahala Mountain	32	Easy
5.	Boulders OHV Area, Lower Loop	48	Easy
16.	Bloody Basin, Sheep Bridge	92	Easy
13.	Gillette Historic Tour	80	Easy
8.	Tule Creek Homestead	60	Moderate
2.	Belmont Mountain	36	Moderate
19.	Sycamore Creek, Sugarloaf Mtn.	104	Moderate
26.	Box Canyon	132	Moderate
3.	Vulture Mountain, Hassayampa River	40	Moderate
14.	New River Canyon	84	Moderate
25.	Montana Mountain	128	Moderate
11.	Dead Cow Gulch	72	Moderate
30.	Walnut Canyon	148	Moderate
24.	Bulldog Canyon	124	Moderate
4.	Wickenburg Mountains	44	Moderate
12.	Black Canyon	76	Moderate
21.	Rolls OHV Area, South	112	Difficult
22.	Saguaro Lake Coves	116	Difficult
29.	Coke Ovens	144	Difficult
7.	Backway to Crown King	56	Difficult
27.	Woodpecker, Ajax Loop	136	Difficult
6.	Boulders OHV Area, Upper Loop	52	Difficult
18.	Log Corral to Bartlett Lake	100	Difficult
17.	Sunflower Mine	96	Difficult
10.	Desoto Mine	68	Difficult
28.	Martinez Canyon	140	Difficult

Trail Ratings Defined

Trail ratings are very subjective. Conditions change for many reasons, including weather and time of year. An easy trail can quickly become difficult when washed out by a rainstorm or blocked by a fallen rock. You must be the final judge of a trail's condition on the day you ride it. If any part of a trail is difficult, the entire trail is rated difficult. You may be able to ride a significant portion of a trail before reaching the difficult spot. Read each trail description carefully for specific information. Turn around when in doubt. Always wear a helmet.

● Easy Trails

Gravel, dirt, clay, sand, or mildly rocky trail or road. Gentle grades. Water levels low except during periods of heavy runoff. Adequate room to pass. Where shelf conditions exist, trail is wide and well maintained with minor sideways tilt. Most trails are passable when wet; however, certain types of clay can become impassable under wet conditions. Smaller, two-wheel-drive ATVs are usually adequate in good weather. Easy trails are best suited for novice riders.

■ Moderate Trails

Rougher and rockier surfaces require slower running speeds. Some riding experience is needed for steeper climbs and descents. Rock-stacking may be necessary to get over the worst spots. Considerable weight shifting may be necessary to offset sideways tilt. Mud can be deep and you may get stuck. Certain types of clay can become impassable when wet. Sand can be soft and steep. Water may be too deep for smaller ATVs. Larger ATVs can usually get through except during periods of heavy runoff. Aggressive tires needed for two-wheel-drive machines. Four-wheel-drive is usually best.

◆ Difficult Trails

Very rough and rocky surfaces require careful tire placement. Slopes may be extremely steep with scary sideways tilt. Skillful riding is necessary to avoid tipping or flipping over. Rock-stacking may be necessary in places, and the worst spots could require assistance from other people. Sand can be very soft and steep. Shelf roads can be very narrow with daunting cliffs. Water and mud can be very deep. Wet clay surfaces can be impassable. Some powerful two-wheel-drive ATVs may get through under good weather conditions, but four-wheel-drive with low-range gearing is highly recommended.

Switchbacks on east side of Montana Mountain, Trail #25, moderate.

INTRODUCTION

Surrounding Phoenix on the west, north and east sides are vast areas of public land ideally suited for riding ATVs, UTVs and dirt bikes. Trails wind across saguaro-covered desert, up steep mountainsides, through rocky canyons, and across sandy stream beds. Along the way, enjoy mountaintop views, historic mines, wildflowers, challenging obstacles, and in some cases, lakeside camp spots.

Most trails can be ridden year around, with the most pleasant weather coming in spring, fall and winter. In the summer, experienced riders head to the high country to escape the desert heat. (For monthly temperature averages, see page 20.)

This book teaches you how to ride responsibly on land controlled by a variety of government land agencies, including the Bureau of Land Management, U.S. Forest Service, Arizona Game and Fish Department, and the Arizona State Land Department. In some cases, special permits are required. They are easy to get and some are free.

The population of Phoenix and its surrounding suburbs is over three million people, which is about half of the population of Arizona.* Motorized recreation is extremely popular in the region. It is hard to drive across town without passing a giant superstore devoted exclusively to power sports products. Heading out of town, many vehicles can be seen hauling ATVs, UTVs, dirt bikes, or a combination of all three.

With all this activity, you might expect trails to be overcrowded. But, with so much land available, we found most trails lightly traveled, and in some cases, seldom saw another rider. The only exception was weekend traffic at Four Peaks Road staging area, which services the very popular Rolls OHV Area. Whatever the situation, this book will show you where to unload and park. In many places, you can camp at the staging area. When this isn't possible, we'll show you where to camp along the trail.

Arizona requires that you title your ATV and meet certain OHV requirements. But Arizona is unique in that you can also register your ATV and ride it on streets, county roads, and highways. In this case, you must be street legal, have a driver's license, and carry proof of insurance. With so many people out on the trails, it is doubly important that everyone understand and follow all laws and regulations. (For complete details of Arizona OHV laws, see page 14.)

* Based on the 2006 U.S. census, the combined population of Phoenix, Glendale, Tempe, Mesa, Scottsdale, Chandler, Peoria and Apache Junction is 3,018,000. The population of Arizona is 6,166,000.

THE BENEFITS OF USING THIS BOOK

We often hear people say, "Why do I need your book? A map is a lot cheaper." Or, "I use the Internet; it's free." These people fail to understand what our books do. Here are the facts:

Maps are great. In fact, we recommend you carry a good one. They give you an overall picture of an area and often provide valuable topographic information. We collected many maps while writing this book. But here's what maps don't do: First, you have to know where the trail is located to know which map to buy. Then, you may have to buy several maps to cover the entire trail. Folding and unfolding the maps can be a hassle. In addition, a map doesn't tell you how difficult the trail is or what surprises may be waiting around the next corner. Maps are often outdated and don't tell you if a route is closed or damaged. Maps usually don't tell you where you can park and unload, or what the camping is like.

The Internet is a valuable tool with an incredible amount of information. We use it extensively to research all the trails in our books. (We especially like "Google Earth." See "Using Google Earth" on page 27.) But we often have to wade through mountains of useless information before we find what we need. After we ride the trails, we find that much of the information is inaccurate or just plain wrong, especially when it comes to directions. Anyone can post information online and no one is held accountable for its accuracy. All too often, you get what you pay for.

The benefits of using this book are many:
- We locate the trails and tell you how to get there.
- We select only the best trails, saving you a boring day.
- We ride every trail ourselves, so you know exactly what to expect. We include lots of photos so you can see it for yourself.
- We rate the trail for difficulty, then tell you what kind of ATV and skills you need to ride the trail.
- We create a custom map for every trail, showing features specific to your needs. The entire trail fits on one convenient page.
- We give you step-by-step trail instructions, conveniently positioned alongside the map.
- We show exact GPS waypoints of key intersections and features.
- We create a locator map which shows the relationship between the trails and gives you an idea how far you'll have to drive.
- We tell you what's good and bad about a trail, without sugar-coating the facts.
- We provide a list of handy addresses and phone numbers.

- We clarify OHV laws specific to your area and advise you on permits required for each trail.
- We advise you on safety, ethics, riding tips, required equipment, trip planning and much more.

Note: Up-to-date trail information can be found on our Web site at www.funtreks.com.

Please note that all the trails in this book were ridden by the authors in the spring of 2008. While trail descriptions and directions were accurate at that time, changes are inevitable. We try to post changes on our Web site as we hear about them, but we don't catch everything. That's why we recommend you check with the appropriate land agencies (BLM, National Forests, etc.) shown on the maps. Addresses and phone numbers are listed in the appendix of this book.

HOW TO USE THIS BOOK

First turn to pages 6 and 7. Page 6 lists each trail with its rating and also shows if the trail is suitable for UTVs. Page 7 has a map which shows you the location of each trail across the state. Author's favorites are shown with an asterisk on page 6.

Each trail in this book has a photo page, a general information page, a directions page and a map page. Read each page carefully before you head out.

The photo page is intended to show you actual trail conditions, not just scenery. Photos include both positive and negative aspects of a trail. A sample of the most difficult spot is usually included. Often photos make the trail look easier than it is. For example, photos of steep spots seldom look as steep as they really are.

The general information page provides directions to the start of the trail, where to unload and camp, difficulty details, highlights, time requirements, length of trail, a basic trail description and location of nearby services.

The directions page and map page work together as one. When the map is turned sideways, so are the directions. The two pages together can be copied (for personal use only) on one 8-1/2″ x 11″ sheet of paper and carried in your pocket while on the trail. The main route, described in the directions, is shown in green, blue or red depending on the difficulty level. This route has a shadow to help it stand out on the page. Other routes nearby are shown in light brown and are not described in the directions. Waypoints for the main route are shown on the directions page while waypoints for other features are shown on the map. Mileage is shown with an overall grid. Check the scale at the bottom of the map because each scale is different.

THE RIGHT TRAIL FOR YOU

It is important to select a trail that matches your riding skills and your equipment. On page 9, you'll find a detailed description of each basic trail rating. Page 8 lists the trails in order of difficulty. Within each category, trails are listed with easiest at the top and hardest at the bottom. Remember that ratings are subjective and can change quickly because of weather and other unforeseen circumstances.

If you are a novice rider, start with the easiest trails at the top of the list on page 8. After mastering basic skills, move down the list. The toughest trails at the bottom are for advanced riders only. Not everyone can attain this level. Don't let others pressure you into riding a trail beyond your skill level. Challenge yourself in small increments. Make sure you read each trail description yourself. Don't rely on others to translate.

ATVs come in all shapes, sizes and horsepower levels. Easy trails can generally be ridden with smaller 2-wheel-drive machines. As trails become more difficult, additional horsepower, 4-wheel drive and low-range gearing become more important. Steep climbs require substantial horsepower. Small ATVs should not be used on difficult trails.

The rating shown on page 6 is for ATVs. Generally, UTVs (60-inch side-by-sides) may find the trails more difficult. Narrow spots are the biggest problem. If it says OK in the far right column, then the trail is suitable for UTVs. If it says "Read," then go to the page indicated and read the complete trail description. You might be able to ride much of the trail before reaching the problem spot.

ARIZONA OHV TITLE & REGISTRATION REQUIREMENTS

Arizona OHV laws are complicated and subject to change at any time. A brochure called *A Guide to Arizona Off-Highway Vehicle Laws, Rules and Regulations,* published by the Arizona Game and Fish Department, does the best job of explaining the laws. However, the brochure does not cover out-of-state ATV usage, nor does it say much about kids riding ATVs. We recommend you get a copy of the brochure and read it yourself. It is your responsibility to know the laws and any changes that may occur. The brochure is available at many locations in Arizona and can be downloaded as a PDF file at: www.azgfd.gov. (Click on "OHV" in green bar and look for "Downloads.")

In an attempt to clarify some of the issues, we spoke to various officials at the Arizona Department of Transportation Motor Vehicle Division (MVD), the Public Information Officer at Game and Fish, and deputies at several county sheriff offices. In one case, we spoke to a deputy who was part of the ATV patrol for Lake Pleasant Regional Park. Our goal was to get a better understanding of the laws and how they might be interpreted by law enforcement in the field. What follows is a compilation of our findings, expressed as simply as possible.

In-state requirements for OHV routes. If you are a resident of Arizona and intend to ride on OHV trails only, you need a title for your ATV and a plate with the letters RV (Recreational Vehicle). This is issued by the Arizona Department of Transportation Motor Vehicle Division. If you buy from a dealer, he will take care of this for you. If you buy from a private party, you need to get the title transferred and get the RV plate yourself. If a lien holder is holding the title, you must prove that you are making the payments. New laws, effective Jan. 1, 2009, will also require an annual sticker for the plate. To ride on OHV trails you will need a spark arrester and a working muffler.

In-state requirements to register your ATV for street use. In Arizona, you can legalize your ATV for street use. For this you need to register your ATV with the MVD and get a plate with the letters MC (Motor Cycle). This plate will also require an annual sticker. To ride on the street, you must have a driver's license and follow all traffic laws. In addition, you must insure your ATV, just like your car. You must carry your driver's license and proof of insurance with you when riding. In addition, your ATV must have the following equipment before it can be registered:

- At least one brake that can be operated by hand or foot.
- Brake light.
- At least one, but not more than two, headlights that shine at least 500 feet ahead.
- At least one taillight visible for at least 500 feet to the rear.
- At least one red rear reflector, if not part of the taillight.
- License plate securely fastened to the rear of the ATV.
- License plate light.
- Wired-in horn audible from distance of 200 feet.
- Working muffler.
- Rearview mirror.
- Seat and footrest for operator
- Fuel tank cap.
- If you live in Phoenix or Tucson metro areas, you may also need to pass an emissions test.

Other OHV laws. Everyone must wear eye protection, regardless of age. Helmets are recommended for everyone, but are not required by law, except for persons 17 years old or younger. You can't ride double on an ATV unless it is manufactured specifically for that purpose. Children cannot ride on streets and highways because, unless they are 16, they can't get a driver's license. However, they can ride on OHV trails. It is recommended that they ride machines matched to their size and body weight. Generally, they should be able to easily straddle the machine with both feet on the foot rests. It is also recommended that children under 14 be supervised by an adult.

Out-of-state rules. Out-of-state visitors must carry proof that they are properly registered or licensed in their home state. With this proof, they can ride on Arizona OHV trails for up to 30 days. After that, they must meet the same requirements as an Arizona resident (see previous page). This creates a complex situation.

Riding on streets and highways, however, is even more complex. According to the Arizona Department of Transportation Motor Vehicle Division, to follow the letter of the law, you cannot ride on streets and highways unless you are registered just like a resident. For this, you need an Arizona address—it's a catch-22.

As a practical matter, since we were not registered in Arizona, here's what we did when faced with the decision to ride on a street or highway. First, we only considered riding on dirt roads. An example would be the Crown King Road that passes through Cleator. Second, we made sure our ATVs were street legal, as much as we could, which in our case meant adding a horn. We also made sure we carried proof of registration, proof of insurance and a valid driver's license from our home state. Our ATVs had all the other requirements except a lighted license plate. Since we couldn't get a plate, it made no sense to add a light. We also don't ride at night. Third, we made sure to obey all traffic laws and to follow proper OHV etiquette. In other words, we demonstrated that we were trying to do the right thing.

Did all this mean we wouldn't get a ticket? No, technically we were still illegal, since we didn't have an "MC" plate. Did it decrease our chance of getting a ticket? Probably. Every law enforcement officer we spoke with said they'd let us keep riding as long as we hadn't been riding longer than 30 days and were obeying all traffic laws.

So, the decision is up to you whether to chance it. Just don't hold us responsible if something goes wrong. Maybe a few letters to the Arizona Department of Transportation might help bring attention to this situation.

Local dust law. Maricopa County, which includes Phoenix and many surrounding areas, in order to meet mandatory EPA requirements, recently passed a law that outlaws the use of OHVs on High

Polution Advisory Days (HPAs). A notice of this law was included in our packet when we applied for our state trust land permit. We questioned many locals and officials about the law, including BLM, NFS and county law enforcement officers. At the time we were in Arizona, we could find no one aware of the law. This left us very confused. We finally found a knowledgeable person at the Arizona Department of Game and Fish, who verified that the law was in effect, but that it is taking time to spread the word. Rest assured, enforcement will eventually begin taking place.

To read full details of this law and to learn what an "HPA" is, go to www.azdeq.gov/environ/air/download/ohv_fact.pdf. To receive a text message on your phone the day before an alert occurs, sign up online at www.azdeq.gov/sms.html. The service is free, but your phone service may charge you for the text message. We signed up for the service and have been receiving messages this last year. One month, in the summer, we had two alerts. A few more alerts were scattered over several months. Expect the number of alerts to increase over time.

State trust land permits. Many trails in Arizona pass through state trust land, where a special permit is required. The permit is good for a year and is good anywhere in Arizona. Arizona residents, who ride on a regular basis, typically purchase the permit every year. If you are visiting from out of state and plan to ride on state trust land, we recommend you get the permit in advance through the mail. For information contact: Arizona State Land Department, 1616 W. Adams, Phoenix, AZ 85007, (602) 542-4631, www.land.state.az.us. (Note: Fees for permits were recently increased.)

Regarding registration and licensing, the same rules apply on state trust land as the rest of Arizona. Make sure you carry the permit with you at all times. No cross-country travel is allowed except for hunters picking up legally killed big game. Don't chase or frighten wildlife. Don't operate your OHV within one-quarter mile of a structure (occupied or not), stock tanks or flood control structures. You don't need a state trust land permit if you already have a valid hunting or fishing license.

NEW FOREST PLANS

All U.S. National Forests are in the process of executing a new plan that requires every forest in the United States to inventory all roads and reevaluate their use. All roads are subject to new designations and final designations will be communicated to the public in the form of a new type of map called an MVUM (Motor Vehicle Use Map). This project has been underway for some time. Some forests are near completion and others are years away. At the time of this writing,

Tonto & Prescott National Forests had not issued any MVUMs.

Motor Vehicle Use Maps. Unlike regular forest maps in color, MVUMs will be black and white. Only roads open to OHV use and a few access roads will appear on the maps. Closed roads will not appear. The maps will be free and readily available. They are designed in a simple way so that there will be less confusion as to which roads and trails are closed and which are open. If a road is not on the map, it is closed. Designation of the roads will not be dependent upon signage. In the past, because signs are often vandalized or removed, people have used this as an excuse to ride on a closed trail. This will no longer fly in the eyes of the law. With designation of the roads no longer in question, plans call for stronger, consistent enforcement.

What about the trails in this book? Since final route designations are not complete as we write this book, we have no way to be sure all the trails shown here will be legal routes when the new plans are released. We've made every attempt to find out and, in some cases, have left out routes that had a higher probability of being closed. We are fairly confident that most of the routes in this book will make the cut, but there is no way to know for sure. Therefore, it is up to you, the reader, to take this into consideration. The MVUM maps will supersede any information contained in this book. As soon as an MVUM becomes available, it is your responsibilty to verify that trails in this book are legal routes. If you are stopped by a law enforcement officer on a newly closed trail, showing him this book will not help a bit.

As information on trail closures becomes available to us, we will try, as quickly as possible, to post this information on our Web site at *www.funtreks.com*. If you know of something closed that is not posted, please send an email to *books@funtreks.com*.

SAFETY TIPS

Helmets. As stated previously, helmets are required by law for riders 17 years old or younger. But frankly, the law should be the least of your concerns. Arizona's rock is very unforgiving. Even a minor incident can cause a serious head injury or even death. Helmets with chin protectors are best.

Body protection. At minimum, wear gloves, long pants, a long-sleeve shirt, heavy leather boots and eye protection (goggles or face guard). If possible, wear a chest protector to avoid being stabbed by a tree branch or other sharp object.

Speed control. Most accidents occur because of excessive speed. Be especially careful around blind curves. Don't follow too close. Leave your lights on all the time.

Fuel limitations. Know how far your ATV will go on a tank of gas. Check your gas level frequently. If you carry extra gas, make sure it is in an approved container.

Riding at night. Avoid it whenever possible. Trails are difficult enough in the daylight. Allow plenty of time for your return trip. Always make sure your lights are working before you head out. You never know when something will delay you.

Stay together. Keep one another in sight to avoid getting split up. Make sure everyone knows the planned route. If you get separated and don't know what to do, wait along the planned route until your party finds you.

Carrying passengers. Unless your ATV is specifically designed for two people, don't carry a passenger. Many ATVs have room for a second person but are not really designed for it. A driver must be able to shift his weight quickly for balance. A second person on the back changes the weight ratio and restricts the driver's movements. This is particularly dangerous on steep slopes. Many people, out of necessity, ride double, but it's not a good practice and is against the law.

Young riders. Riders under the age of 14 should be supervised by a responsible adult at all times. Riders should be tall enough to straddle their machines with both feet on footrests with a slight bend at the knees. Most injuries to children are caused by riding machines too large for their small bodies.

Be alert. Make sure you are well rested. It's a crime to ride while under the influence of alcohol or drugs.

Tell someone your plans. Always tell someone where you are going and when you plan to return. Leave a map of your route. Make sure you tell them when you return so they don't go out looking for you.

Travel with another vehicle. Walking out can be grueling and dangerous. In an emergency, a second vehicle could save a life.

Flash floods. Arizona is usually dry; however, storms can move in quickly, bringing a chance of flash floods. A dry stream bed can become a raging torrent in minutes. Wait for water to recede before attempting to cross. If water starts to fill a wash or canyon, exit perpendicular to the water flow. If necessary, leave your ATV and climb to safety. Don't try to outrun rising water.

Clay surface roads. Some roads may contain clay that can be very slippery or even impassable when wet. Stay off these roads if rain is imminent.

Changing conditions. Arizona's backcountry is fragile and under constant assault by forces of nature and man. Rock slides can occur or an entire road can be washed away overnight. A trail may be closed without notice. Be prepared to face unexpected situations.

Lightning. During a storm, stay away from lone trees, cliff edges and high points. The rubber tires of your ATV can act as an insulator between you and the ground, but stay low. Lightning can strike from a distant storm even when it's clear overhead. Seek shelter whenever possible.

Mines, tunnels and caves. Be careful around old mine buildings. Stay out of mines, tunnels and caves. They may look safe, but noxious gases may be present. Don't let children or pets play in these areas.

Altitude sickness. Some people may experience altitude sickness on mountain trails. Symptoms include nausea, dizziness, headaches or weakness. This condition usually improves over time. To minimize symptoms, give yourself time to acclimate, drink plenty of fluids, decrease salt intake, reduce alcohol and caffeine, eat foods high in car-bohydrates and try not to exert yourself.

PHOENIX WEATHER STATISTICS

Month	Avg. High	Avg. Low	Warmest Ever	Coldest Ever	Avg. Precip.
January	66	41	88	17	0.8 in.
February	70	44	92	22	0.6 in.
March	75	49	100	25	0.9 in.
April	84	55	105	32	0.3 in.
May	93	64	113	40	0.1 in.
June	103	72	122	50	0.1 in.
July	105	80	121	61	0.8 in.
August	103	79	116	60	1.0 in.
September	99	72	118	47	0.7 in.
October	88	61	107	34	0.6 in.
November	75	48	93	25	0.6 in.
December	66	42	88	22	0.9 in.

TRIP PREPARATION

Think ahead. You probably can't prepare for every possible thing that can go wrong, but thinking about it ahead of time will improve your chances. Here are a few things to consider:

Vehicle readiness. Inspect and service your ATV regularly. Check belts, tires, battery, spark plug(s), fluids, lights and worn parts. If you don't do your own mechanical work, pay a qualified person to do it.

Know your ATV. It goes without saying, you must know how to operate your own ATV. If renting or borrowing equipment, make sure you are well instructed on its operation. If traveling with a group, share idiosyncrasies of each other's machines.

Check for trail closures. Call the BLM or Forest Service to find out if any trails are damaged or closed. Keep in mind, they may not be aware of damage if it occurred recently. (See contact information in appendix.)

Prepare for an overnight stay. It is not unusual to get stuck on a trail overnight. You'll rest easier if you are prepared.

Check the weather forecast. Weather can make or break your day.

CHECKLIST OF EQUIPMENT AND SUPPLIES

It's daunting to list everything you might need on a trip. Where do you put it all? Try to miniaturize as much as possible. Check your ATV specifications for weight limits and distribute weight correctly front and rear. Everything should be securely tied down or in a carry box.

Basics:
- Water (Carry at least one gallon per person per day.)
- High-energy foods like Cliff bars
- Warm raincoat
- Small space blanket
- Small shovel
- Large trash bags (can be used for trash or rain protection)
- Map, compass (See map suggestions in this introduction.)
- Basic tool kit (Our ATVs came with a tiny tool kit.)
- Tow strap
- Waterproof matches or magnesium fire-starter
- Small flashlight (Maglites double as a candle.)
- Small first aid kit and water purification tablets
- Toilet paper, sunscreen, insect repellent, pencil and paper
- Knife or multi-purpose tool
- Extra ignition key, prescription glasses, medications

Other things you may want:
- Tire repair plug kit or can of tire sealant
- CO2 cartridge gun or hand air pump (We carry an electric pump that plugs into 12-volt socket.)
- Extra clothing, gloves, coat if going into the mountains
- More complete set of tools (see suggestions below)
- Larger first aid kit with instruction book
- Small ice chest or insulated bag, larger choice of foods, drinks
- Sleeping bag, small tent

- Water purification filter
- Large plastic tarp, nylon cords
- Signal mirror, whistle, flare gun
- Small set jumper cables
- Extra gas, oil, fluids
- Small fire extinguisher
- Baling wire, duct tape, nylon zip ties and string
- Extra spark plug(s)
- Extra headlight bulb
- Small assortment of nuts, bolts, clamps and cotter pins
- Small axe or hatchet or folding saw
- Cell phone (Regular cell phone is not reliable but take it anyway. Satellite phone is best if you can afford one.)
- Small handheld CB radio or UHF radio
- GPS unit with solid mount
- Camera
- Extra batteries
- Winch or small come-along
- Portable toilet (lightweight bag type) where required
- Firewood (if camping where wood collection is prohibited)

Suggested tools:
- Open end/box wrenches (check ATV for sizes)
- Small socket set (check ATV for sizes)
- Small adjustable wrench
- Combination screwdriver with different tips
- Spark plug wrench
- Needle-nose pliers with wire cutter, Vise-Grips
- Any special tools required for your ATV
- Low pressure tire gauge

YOUR RESPONSIBILITIES AS A BACKCOUNTRY RIDER

More and more visitors are coming to Arizona every year. They come for many different reasons, including hiking, biking, rafting, fishing, hunting, camping, rock hounding, Jeeping, ATV riding, dirt-bike riding and general sightseeing. Most of these visitors spend at least part of their time in the backcountry. The accumulated result of these large numbers is having a negative effect on the countryside. Hiking and biking trails are widening with more shortcuts appearing. Camp spots are increasing in number and getting bigger. More trash is blowing around and vegetation is being trampled. But worst of all is the proliferation of tire tracks across pristine land. It begins with one selfish or ignorant individual who cuts across an open area. The next person uses these tracks as an excuse to claim a road exists. Before long a new road is formed. Eventually the hillsides are covered with a spaghetti-like network of roads to nowhere.

It has been my observation, in the many years I've been traveling in the backcountry, that the majority of backcountry travelers are well-meaning, responsible people who do their best to follow the rules by staying on what they know are legal routes. Frankly, I've never personally witnessed someone deliberate cut across a fragile open area. If I did, I'd do my best to report them immediately. I have seen people widen a trail by going around a mud hole or pulling over at a narrow spot to let someone pass. In these cases, I kindly explain why this should not be done. Obviously, there are people doing damage, but I believe it is a small percentage. Unfortunately, it doesn't take many irresponsible people to spoil it for everyone else.

The BLM, National Forest Service and Arizona Game and Fish Department are responsible for most of the backcountry around Phoenix, and are working hard to educate land users. Too often, however, their efforts are failing. Sometimes their only recourse is to completely close an area, much to the chagrin of the majority of people who are acting responsibly.

With that as a prelude, here is a list of your responsibilities as a backcountry rider:

Stay on existing routes. If you are not sure a road is legal, it probably isn't. Designated routes are unquestionably well traveled even though route markers may be illegally removed. If you stay on the routes in this book, you are more likely to be legal.

Leaving the trail causes unnecessary erosion, kills vegetation and spoils the beauty of the land. Scars remain for years. Don't widen the trail by riding around rocks and muddy spots. Don't take shortcuts or cut across switchbacks. When you have to pass another vehicle, wait for a wide spot. Anticipate where you will pull over when you see an oncoming vehicle. Pull over at wide spots to let faster vehicles pass.

Wilderness areas and national parks. Boundaries for these areas are usually well marked. Riding inside these areas is a very serious offense.

Stay off single-track trails. Nothing is more upsetting to a dirt biker or mountain biker than to have the trail widened by an ATV. Do not ride on single-track routes.

Private property. Some trails in this book are public roads that cross private property. These roads are usually well marked. As you pass through, you must stay on the road. You are trespassing anywhere else. Respect the rights of property owners. Pass through quietly, don't disturb livestock and leave gates the way you find them unless signs say otherwise.

Ruins and archaeological sites. It is a federal crime to disturb historical and archaeological sites. This includes petroglyphs and pictographs. Please admire them from a distance and take only pictures.

Trash disposal. Carry bags and pack out your trash. Make an extra effort to pick up litter left by others.

Human waste. The disposal of human waste and toilet paper is becoming a big problem in the backcountry where facilities are not provided. Keep a small shovel handy and bury solid waste 6 to 12 inches deep, away from trails, campsites and at least 300 feet from any water source, which includes dry washes. Put toilet paper and hygiene products in a small plastic bag and dispose with trash. (Consider commercial Wag Bags®. See at www.thepett.com.)

Camping. Generally, BLM and Forest Service camping guidelines allow dispersed camping along the trails. These spots are free, but no services are provided. In some places, camping is restricted to designated sites. Here, you may find metal fire rings, toilets and sometimes picnic tables. Payment is made via self-service fee stations.

When selecting a dispersed campsite along the trail, you can usually find a place where others have already camped. Often, rock fire rings have already been built. Do everything you can to avoid camping in a new spot. Rules for dispersed camping include a 14-day limit, packing out your trash, staying 100 feet away from water sources and not leaving campfires unattended. Always make sure your fire is dead out. Douse it thoroughly until it is cold to the touch. In addition, follow these low-impact camping techniques:

- Don't burn cans, bottles, etc. in your campfire.
- Use only dead and downed wood where collection is allowed.
- Use a fire pan whenever possible. (This is a metal tray, like a garbage can lid, that holds ashes, which when cooled can be carried away with your trash.)
- Heat water for cleaning rather than using soap.
- If possible, use a propane stove for cooking. It's quick, easy and better for the environment.
- Don't trample vegetation around the campsite. This causes the campsite to gradually enlarge until it becomes one huge bare area. And above all, don't let the kids ride their ATVs around the campsite.

COURTESY AND ETHICS

Riding an ATV in Arizona's backcountry is fun. On many trails, you can ride for hours without seeing another person. The most popular trails, however, will be shared with other riders, hikers, bikers and horseback riders, most of whom are looking for quiet and solitude. Obviously, there is an inherent conflict when ATVs cross paths with non-motorized users.

When we are on the trail, we do our best to mitigate the situation. We recognize that, although our ATVs are quieter than most, they still make noise, which is going to irritate some people. We realize our riding kicks up dust and that, if we don't slow down, somebody's going to get upset. Since we hike and bike ourselves, it's easy to empathize with their situation. It's even more critical when animals are involved. We certainly don't want to run over anyone's dog or spook their horse.

The title "Courtesy and Ethics" suggests that the following actions are voluntary. In theory, that may be. In practice, however, following these suggestions is critical to the long-term survival of motorized recreation. Fair or not, OHV recreation has a tarnished image. We must all do our best to improve that image.

Overtaking hikers. Slow down well in advance to give time for your dust to settle. Swing wide and pass as slowly as possible. If they have a dog or pack animal, give them time to prepare. You may have to stop completely and shut off your engine. Every situation is different. Allow them an opportunity to give you instructions.

Oncoming hikers. On a wide road, move way over and go by as slowly as possible. On a narrower trail, pull over, shut off your engine and wait for them to walk by. Take off your helmet and exchange courtesies whenever possible. If they have a dog or pack animal, pull over sooner and stop until they are well past before starting your engine.

Overtaking horseback riders. This is the trickiest of all situations. You have to get close enough so they hear you, but not so close to spook the horses. Some horses stand quietly, others may bolt at the slightest provocation. You might have to stop, shut off your engine and walk toward the riders to discuss the situation. They may want to dismount or ride way off to the side. If they ignore you and you are sure they know you are behind them, proceed as cautiously as possible.

Oncoming horseback riders. Pull over, as early as possible, shut off your engine and wait for them to pass. Take off your helmet and exchange greetings.

Mountain bikers. With slow-moving bikers, you handle the situation much the same as hikers. However, it gets more complicated when the bikers are riding fast. If you gradually catch up to them, you might want to slow down a bit and not pass at all. If you can't wait, make sure they know you are behind them, then go just fast enough to get by. You don't want to go too fast, but you don't want to dally beside them either. If bikers approach you from behind, just slow down and let them pass. A smile and a wave really help.

Making your ATV quieter. If you have a loud machine, ask your ATV dealer for suggestions to make it quieter. Make sure the muffler is working properly. Whatever you do, don't alter your existing muffler to make it louder.

Wildlife. It's a crime to harass wild animals. Deer are the most frequent critters you'll see, but many other animals abound. Most scurry off before you know they're there, but sometimes you get lucky and they hang around long enough to snap a picture. Watch for Gila Monsters crossing the road. We saw several during our visit.

Carry extra water for others: This is a personal thing that we like to do. We've been able to help some desperate people over the years. Most often it's bikers who have underestimated their needs.

RECOMMENDED MAPS

Route-finding in Arizona's backcountry can be very challenging. Before you head out, make sure you have a good map of the area. The maps in this book will direct you along the described route, but if you get lost, you'll want a detailed map of the entire area. Here is a list of the maps we used during our trip:

- DeLorme Atlas & Gazetteer. This atlas covers the entire state in significant detail. No matter where you go, you have a map that will get you home. It's cheap and very handy.
- Tonto and Prescott National Forests. Both of these maps are fairly up to date.
- Tonto National Forest, Cave Creek Ranger District
- BLM map of Agua Fria National Monument
- BLM Access Guide, Lake Pleasant/ Hieroglyphic Mountains
- Desert Wells Off-Highway Recreation Guide, by Arizona Game and Fish Department.
- Off-Highway Vehicle Recreation Guide for Arizona, by Arizona State Parks
- Rolls OHV Area. Online map that we printed out from the Arizona Game and Fish Web site, www.azgfd.gov. (Click on OHV in the green bar, then select "Trails & Places to Ride." This takes you to a long list of riding areas, including Rolls OHV Area. Some areas include maps. These maps are not detailed.)

Using Google Earth. A new tool has emerged in the last few years that is fantastic for backcountry travelers. It is called "Google Earth" and the software can be downloaded free from the Internet. It enables you to see detailed pictures of almost anywhere on earth. In many places (not all), the detail is so fine, you can clearly see all the trails and roads on which you will be traveling. You can also print out the area and use it like a map. After your trip, you can download tracklogs and waypoints (using .gpx files) to see where you went. In addition, you have the option of showing a 3-dimensional view, which can be looked at from any angle. You can study the area before you go and revisit the area from your computer.

Other route-finding tips. Watch for cairns (small stacks of rocks) that often mark the trail. They may be knocked over, but you can still recognize them if you pay attention. Sometimes colored ribbons are tied to tree limbs or bushes to mark the trail. Look for tire marks and oil drippings on steep rock surfaces.

GLOBAL POSITIONING

Consider buying a GPS unit if you haven't done so already. Prices have really come down and they've become quite simple to use. The unit doesn't have to be fancy, just good enough to provide accurate coordinates. When used with *DeLorme's Atlas*, you can easily figure out where you are. More expensive GPS units have built-in maps and allow you to download and upload information into your computer. You would probably like these features, too, but they are not necessary.

We used GPS while working on this book. Frankly, we've found it to be an indispensable tool. We didn't know how well our unit *(Garmin 76CSx)* would work with the jarring and inclement weather, but it worked flawlessly. Newer and better models are now available. We plug the power cord into a 12-volt power socket and never worry about batteries. At the end of the day, we download the tracklogs and waypoints into the computer and print out the entire route on mapping software, e.g., Mapsource, National Geographic Topo, or Google Earth. (See appendix for listing of main GPS companies. For free file conversion, go to www.gpsbabel.org)

GPS Settings. All the trails in this book show key GPS waypoints in Latitude/Longitude format in hours/minutes.hundredths of minutes. Don't confuse this format with hours/minutes/seconds which looks similar. Make sure your GPS unit displays in the same format or your readings will appear in error. Set your Datum on WGS 84 or NAD83 (not NAD27).

DESERT SURVIVAL

Self-reliance. Most of us live in populated areas and are accustomed to having other people around when things go wrong. In Arizona's remote backcountry, you must be self-reliant. Don't count on anyone else's help.

Take plenty of water. We can't stress enough the importance of carrying and drinking plenty of water—at least one gallon per person per day. Running out of water can be a fatal mistake.

Avoid hottest part of day. On long summer days, try to ride in the morning and evening to avoid the hottest part of the day, or head to the high country.

First Aid. Always carry a good first-aid kit. Take a first-aid course and learn the basics. Make sure the kit contains first-aid instructions.

What to do if you have mechanical problems or you get lost. Stay with your ATV. There's always a chance that someone will come along if you stay near the road. Your ATV is easier to see than you are. Seek shade. You're more likely to find a rock overhang than a shady tree. Don't sit on the hot ground. Dig down to cooler sand below. Create your own shade with blankets or a tarp. Drink plenty of water; don't wait until you get thirsty. Wear light-colored, loose-fitting clothing that covers as much of your skin as possible. Wear a hat and use sunscreen. Collect firewood before dark. Build a fire before you need it. If you get lost or separated from your group, stay in one place.

If you're familiar with the area and know exactly how far it is to hike out and are absolutely sure you can make it, consider walking out. Cover up with loose clothing, take plenty of water, food, and rain protection to stay dry. As a last resort, travel at night when it's cooler if the terrain is not too treacherous. Make sure you can see where you're walking.

Try to draw attention to yourself using a whistle or signal mirror. Creating a smoky fire is a difficult thing to do in the desert, but this method could be used as a last resort.

If you have a cell phone, try to find a point where you can get a signal and call for help. If you have a medical emergency, call 911. Carry a satellite phone if you can afford one.

Hyperthermia. When your body overheats it's called hyperthermia. Symptoms include dry, flushed skin, inability to sweat, rapid heartbeat, and a rising body temperature. Hyperthermia is often preceded by cramps. They may not go away by drinking water alone. You may need food or salt. If hyperthermia is allowed to progress, you could collapse from heatstroke, which is extremely serious and can be fatal if not treated quickly.

To prevent hyperthermia, stay in the shade, don't overexert yourself, wear loose-fitting clothing, and drink plenty of water. If work is required, conserve your energy as best as possible.

Dehydration. As your body sweats to cool itself, it dehydrates. You may be drinking water but not enough. Eating may make you nauseous. You won't want to eat or drink. As symptoms get worse, your mouth will become dry, you may become dizzy, develop a headache, and become short of breath. At some point, you may not be able to walk or care for yourself.

You must prevent dehydration before it happens. Drink more than just to quench your thirst. If you must conserve water, rest as much as possible, try not to sweat, and don't eat a lot. Digestion requires body fluids. If you have plenty of water, drink it.

Hypothermia. It gets cold in the desert after the sun goes down. If it rains and gets windy, you could find yourself shivering in no time, especially if you've worked up a sweat during the day. Your hands and feet will become stiff. You may not be able to hold a match and start a fire. Prevention is the key. Put on a jacket before you begin to get cold. Stay dry. Change clothes if necessary. If you get too cold, blankets may not be enough to warm you. Build a fire, drink hot liquids, or cuddle up with someone else.

FINAL COMMENTS

We've made every effort to make this book as accurate and as easy to use as possible. If you have ideas for improvements or find any significant errors, please write to us at FunTreks, Inc., P.O. Box 3127, Monument, CO 80132-3127. Or e-mail to *books@funtreks.com*. Whether you're a novice or expert, we hope this book makes your backcountry experience safer, easier, and more fun.

Map Legend

Interstate

Paved Road

Unpaved Road

Easy Trail

Moderate Trail

Difficult Trail

Other Trails

Detailed Directions
(Indicated with shadow)

Hiking Trail

Boundaries

MONTANA MTN.   Mountain Peak

Lake, River

Map Orientation

17   Interstate

50   U.S. Highway

35   State & County Road

700   Forest Service Road

Start   Starting point of trail

Public Toilet

Gas, Service

Parking

Staging Area

Picnic Area

Camping Area

Mine

Hiking Trailhead

Water Crossing

Bridge

Windmill, Water

Scenic Point

Rock Art

Archaeological Site, Ruin

Fishing

Cabin

Major Obstacle

05   GPS Waypoint

NO ATVs

THE TRAILS

Descending toward Saguaro Lake through Rolls OHV Area, Trail #21.

View from summit. Picnic tables and plenty of parking. Historic observatory on right.

Wild flowers in mid March.

Old mining camp on side trip.

All routes wide enough for UTVs.

Steep, twisting road is fun to ride.

Harquahala Mountain 1

Getting There: Take I-10 west from Phoenix to Exit 81 (About 47 miles from the 101 loop). Head northwest on Salome Road for 9.6 miles and turn right on Eagle Eye Road. Continue north 8.5 miles and turn left at large sign for Harquahala Mountain Byway. Drive in short distance to staging area on right.

Staging/Camping: Large staging area with plenty of room to park equipped with picnic tables, fire rings, a modern vault toilet, a covered information kiosk and an unloading ramp for pickup trucks. Not sure whether camping is allowed here, but saw no signs to the contrary. Camping is allowed at several places farther down the road (see map).

Difficulty: Main route is relatively easy, although as you near the top, its gets steeper and rockier. Side trip to mine at Waypoint 02 is short but very steep and rocky. Side trip at Waypoint 04 is mostly moderate, but has a couple of steep, rocky spots.

Highlights: A BLM National Byway which climbs to the top of 5,681-ft. Harquahala Peak, the highest mountain in southwestern Arizona. At the top, find an observatory built by the Smithsonian Institution in use from 1920 to 1925. Information panels explain the history. You'll find picnic tables and plenty of parking room—a great spot for lunch. Large solar collectors at the top are used by the Central Arizona Project.

Time & Distance: Round trip on main road takes 2 to 3 hours. Add 1 to 2 hours for side trips.

Trail Description: You'll move along quickly on the lower portion of trail because it is relatively straight and flat. As you climb, frequent twists and turns require slower speeds and more caution. A very steep section near the top has been prone to erosion in the past. This created unpredictable and sometimes difficult conditions. This short section has now been paved, making for a quick and easy climb. The optional side trip at the top splits two ways. Right deadends at a scenic overlook; left drops downhill to an old mining camp with several interesting stone cabins.

Services: Gas and restaurant at Tonopah, Exit 94 off Interstate 10.

Directions: *(Shadowed portion of trail is described here.)*

WP	Mile	Action
01	**0.0**	*N33° 43.77´ W113° 17.80´* Head northwest from staging area on a well-maintained dirt road.
	2.3	First of two camp spots on right. Each spot has picnic table and metal fire ring.
02	**3.5**	*N33° 45.83´ W113° 19.71´* Bear left uphill on most traveled road. (Lesser road to right leads to a small mining camp with a stone cabin. Continue past cabin on steep, difficult road to mine and ore chute. Experienced riders only.)
	5.4	Road gets steeper as it climbs several long switchbacks, then levels out again. Views improve as you steadily climb.
03	**8.7**	*N33° 48.48´ W113° 21.27´* Steepest section of trip is paved a short distance to minimize erosion.
04	**9.6**	*N33° 48.43´ W113° 20.77´* Continue uphill on main road as it curves left. (Lesser road to right drops downhill and forks. Right at fork dead ends at an overlook. Left at fork drops downhill to an abandoned mining camp with stone cabins.)
	9.9	First parking lot on right as you near summit. Great views from picnic table in corner of parking lot. A second smaller parking lot follows immediately. Here you'll find more picnic tables and a hiking path with information panels that explain the history of the observatory.
05	**10.0**	*N33° 48.71´ W113° 20.81´* Arrive at summit dominated by cell towers and large solar panels. Road continues a short distance past summit.

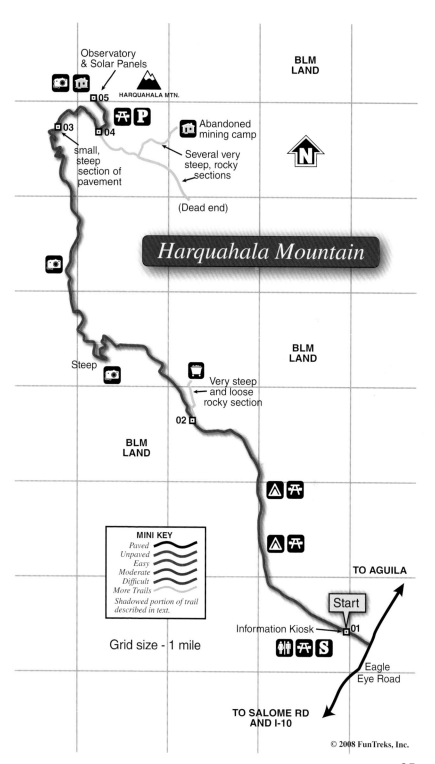

Observatory
& Solar Panels

HARQUAHALA MTN.

BLM
LAND

□ 05

[P]

□ 03   □ 04

small,
steep
section of
pavement

Abandoned
mining camp

Several very
steep, rocky
sections

N

(Dead end)

Harquahala Mountain

Steep

BLM
LAND

Very steep
and loose
rocky section

02 □

BLM
LAND

MINI KEY

Paved
Unpaved
Easy
Moderate
Difficult
More Trails

*Shadowed portion of trail
described in text.*

Grid size - 1 mile

TO AGUILA

Start

Information Kiosk ——□ 01

[S]

Eagle
Eye Road

TO SALOME RD
AND I-10

© 2008 FunTreks, Inc.

View from bridge over Arizona Project Canal.

Many mine adits; do not enter.

Looking south from Belmont Mine beyond foundations of old stamp mill.

Main shaft at Morning Star Mine. Stay back.

Difficult spot on optional exit route.

Abandoned windmill north of Belmont Mtn.

Probably used to store explosives.

Belmont Mountain

Getting There: From Phoenix, head west on Interstate 10 to Exit 98 (about 35 miles from the 101 loop). From exit, head north to Indian School Road and turn left. Go west 1 mile and turn right on 387th Avenue. After another 3.5 miles, pavement ends. Continue straight a short distance and follow road left onto dusty Northern Avenue. Continue west another mile to T intersection, then turn right. After 0.1 miles, bear left heading slightly northwest. Ignore side roads until you reach bridge over the Arizona Project Canal (another 2.5 miles). Continue 0.2 miles to intersection in open area that marks start of trail.

Staging/Camping: Although there is no defined staging area, you'll find adequate room to park and unload near the start of trail. You may also choose to park along the road at wide spots and ride your ATV to the start. Most of the adjoining land is private residential, but unoccupied; however, be aware that you may be parking on private property. Make sure you pull over far enough to not block the road.

Difficulty: Most of this route is easy; however, as you approach Belmont Mountain, the road gets steeper and is partly washed out in places. Lesser side roads have difficult challenges. An optional route that loops back to start has one difficult spot (see photo at left).

Highlights: A remote, high-desert, mountainous area with many old mining roads. Very scenic when viewed from high vantage points. Stay clear of open vertical mine shafts and never enter mines.

Time & Distance: Less than 5 miles from start to Belmont Mountain, but the main road continues north another 6 miles. You can spend most of a day exploring the area. If you are a skilled rider, add challenge by returning south over optional loop route.

Trail Description: Pass through sparsely populated residential area and cross lone bridge over the Arizona Project Canal. Continue north across remote desert and ascend Belmont Mountain on roughening road. Explore network of old mining roads that crisscross the rough, mountainous area or stay on main road as it continues north towards Wickenburg. Return to start via more difficult optional loop.

Services: Gas and restaurant west on I-10 at Tonopah, Exit 94.

Directions: *(Shadowed portion of trail is described here.)*

WP	Mile	Action
01	**0.0**	*N33° 35.33´ W112° 55.26´* Continue northwest on wide, gravel road.
	0.9	Bear right.
	1.4	Bear left.
02	**2.6**	*N33° 37.25´ W112° 56.43´* Bear right.
	2.9	Cross cattle guard and go by delapidated metal water tank on left.
	4.2	Road begins to climb towards Belmont Mountain and is heavily rutted in spots. Use caution as conditions may have worsened since time of this writing.
03	**4.5**	*N33° 38.59´ W112° 55.81´* Main road continues straight. (Left here goes to Belmont Mine on south face of mountain. Road is blocked to motorized vehicles part way up.)
04	**4.7**	*N33° 38.68´ W112° 55.67´* Main road continues north towards Wickenburg and gets easier. Left circles around back side of Belmont Mountain to other mines. Right goes to Morning Star Mine, which can be seen on hillside looking east. (To take optional loop back to start, turn right at Waypoint 04 and go 0.25 miles to 4-way intersection, then turn right downhill and follow narrow shelf road south past the Morning Star Mine. Steep, rocky and difficult road continues downhill past mine into dry wash, and eventually becomes easy most of the way back to start.)

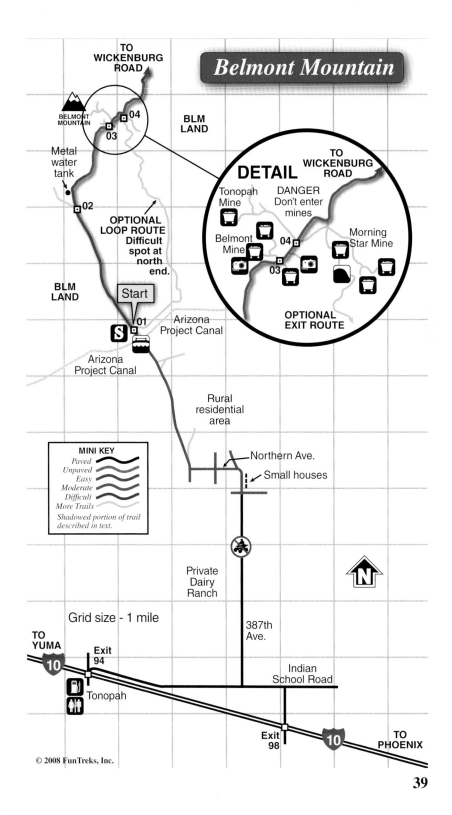

Belmont Mountain

TO WICKENBURG ROAD

BELMONT MOUNTAIN

BLM LAND

Metal water tank

02

OPTIONAL LOOP ROUTE
Difficult spot at north end.

BLM LAND

Start

01

Arizona Project Canal

Arizona Project Canal

DETAIL

TO WICKENBURG ROAD

Tonopah Mine

DANGER Don't enter mines

Belmont Mine

04

03

Morning Star Mine

OPTIONAL EXIT ROUTE

Rural residential area

Northern Ave.

Small houses

MINI KEY
Paved
Unpaved
Easy
Moderate
Difficult
More Trails
Shadowed portion of trail described in text.

Private Dairy Ranch

Grid size - 1 mile

387th Ave.

N

TO YUMA

10

Exit 94

Tonopah

Indian School Road

Exit 98

10

TO PHOENIX

© 2008 FunTreks, Inc.

Unload at staging area next to sandy river bed.

Danger! Open mine shafts.

Trails are fairly wide but fun.

Red Cliffs along the river 1.8 miles south.

You'll go by this roofless stone cabin early in the ride.

Vulture Mtn. Hassayampa Riv. ⬛3

Getting There: From Phoenix, head northwest on Highway 60. Turn left on Gates Road at mile marker 121 and head west. Bear right at large fork at 1.4 miles. Staging area is on left next to river at 2.3 miles.

Staging/Camping: Unload on east side of river. No signs mark the staging area, but you'll find plenty of open space to park between the tamarisk overgrowth. No facilities are provided. Pack out your trash.

Difficulty: Mostly hard-packed dirt with occasional rocky sections. A few steep climbs and descents give the trail its moderate rating. A large number of trails crisscross the area, which makes route-finding confusing at times. BEWARE: Trail passes through mining areas with dangerous open mine shafts. Do not ride off main trail and be careful where you walk. Keep an eye on your kids.

Highlights: A widespread trail system meanders across undulating desert and low foothills. Area is very remote and sees little traffic—a great place to ride if you're tired of crowds. Ride north and south for many miles along the sandy Hassayampa River bed. See interesting Red Cliffs just 1.8 miles south of the staging area.

Time & Distance: Allow about 3 hours for 14.4-mile loop described here. Extend trip by exploring numerous side trails.

Trail Description: Gate to start of trail is on the west side of the Hassayampa River, which is typically just a dry, sandy wash. Leave staging area and head due west until you see road on the other side. Follow road west a couple of miles, then branch north to begin a wide loop. Pay close attention to directions as numerous roads branch off. You'll pass a roofless stone cabin, then several mining areas where dangerous open mine shafts are just a few yards away from the trail. Trail winds its way through varied desert terrain and circles back to start. Once back at the Hassayampa River, head south along the sandy river bed to Red Cliffs. You can continue many more miles; however, opening and closing numerous cattle gates becomes tedious. If you have the patience, you can ride south all the way to Interstate 10, about 28 miles.

Services: Closest gas is about 10 miles north on Highway 60 on the south side of Wickenburg. Nothing in Morristown.

Directions: *(Shadowed portion of trail is described here.)*

WP	Mile	Action
01	0.0	N33° 51.11′ W112° 39.54′ Head west from staging area across Hassayampa River bed.
02	0.2	N33° 51.16′ W112° 39.79′ Pass through gate on west bank of river. Continue west on main trail as you pass lesser roads.
	0.4	Bear left uphill on main trail.
03	2.0	N33° 51.40′ W112° 41.42′ Bear right on lesser road heading north. You will cross a wash shortly after the turn.
	2.7	Continue straight as road joins from right.
	2.9	Bear left.
	3.1	Cross wide wash.
04	3.3	N33° 52.30′ W112° 41.52′ Bear left.
	3.7	Steep hill. Stay to your right when coming down.
	4.0	Roofless stone cabin on right.
05	4.5	N33° 52.85′ W112° 42.27′ Hard left turn out of wash, then left at next T intersection.
	4.7	Bear left, following more traveled road.
	5.3	Continue straight. (Lesser road to left connects to network of other trails back to start.)

WP	Mile	Action
06	5.5	N33° 52.69′ W112° 43.09′ Bear right out of wash. Watch for open mine shafts to your left and right for the next 1.5 miles.
	6.2	Pass through gate and close it.
07	7.0	N33° 52.80′ W112° 44.12′ Bear left heading south on lesser traveled road. (Continuing straight will make a big loop and eventually bring you back to wpt 08.)
	7.5	Wildlife water collection station on left. Keep out.
08	8.4	N33° 51.68′ W112° 44.51′ Bear left at T intersection.
	9.4	Bear left on more traveled road.
09	9.8	N33° 51.05′ W112° 43.50′ Pass through gate and bear left at major T intersection. Follow the trail into a wash and take a right, then make an immediate left out of the wash.
	10.0	Continue straight on most traveled trail.
	11.0	Continue straight through intersection. This high point is a good spot for pictures.
	11.7	Continue straight as you join major road.
03	12.4	Return to point where loop started. Straight goes back to start.

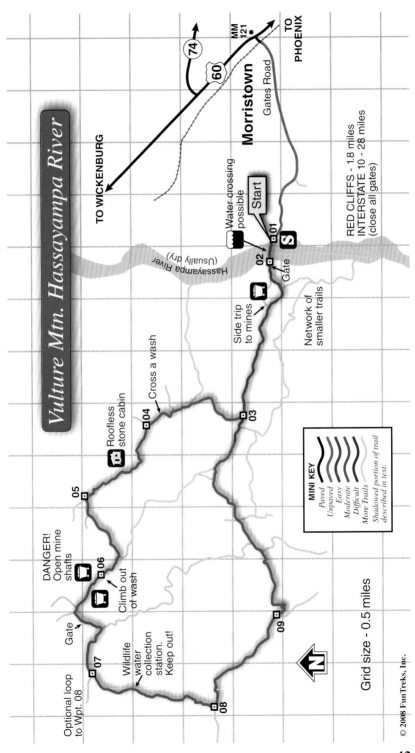

Vulture Mtn. Hassayampa River

TO WICKENBURG

TO PHOENIX

Morristown

Gates Road

MM 121

74

60

RED CLIFFS - 1.8 miles
INTERSTATE 10 - 28 miles
(close all gates)

Water-crossing possible

Start

01

S

Gate

02

Hassayampa River (Usually dry)

Side trip to mines

Network of smaller trails

Cross a wash

Roofless stone cabin

04

03

05

DANGER! Open mine shafts

06

Climb out of wash

Gate

Wildlife water collection station. Keep out!

07

Optional loop to Wpt. 08

08

09

MINI KEY
Paved
Unpaved
Easy
Moderate
Difficult
More Trails
Shadowed portion of trail described in text.

N

Grid size - 0.5 miles

© 2008 FunTreks, Inc.

43

Important left turn at Waypoint 02.

Several gates along the route.

Very steep in spots; novice riders beware.

Bradshaw's Grave is well marked.

Remains at Copperopolis.

Scenic spot near end of trail.

Wickenburg Mountains 4

Getting There: From Phoenix, head northwest on Highway 60 towards Wickenburg. As you come into Wickenburg, turn right on El Recreo Drive 0.3 miles after mile marker 11. (If you miss El Recreo Drive, turn just before McDonald's Restaurant. This road also runs into Constellation Road.) El Recreo Drive becomes Constellation Road, and the pavement soon ends. Stay right where Blue Tank Road goes left. Stay left at 4.2 miles where an unmarked road goes right. Stay on the main road another 4 miles until you see sign for Buckhorn Road on right.

Staging/Camping: Best staging area is on left just across from start of Buckhorn Road at 8.7 miles. (Drive in at least 4.2 miles before considering any other places to unload.)

Difficulty: Several steep, rocky spots that require good balance and careful tire placement. Not recommended for novice riders. Best done with a 4-wheel-drive ATV.

Highlights: Visit the well-marked grave of Isaac Bradshaw, namesake of the Bradshaw Mountains. Great mountain views in a truly remote setting. Trail ends at historic Copperopolis Townsite. Numerous other mines along the route. For in-depth mining history and memorabilia, visit the museum in Wickenburg.

Time & Distance: Just under 9 miles from Highway 60 to Buckhorn Road. Constellation Road is well maintained, but can be washed out after storms. Another 16 miles from start of Buckhorn Road to end of trail at Copperopolis Townsite. Allow 6-7 hours for round trip.

Trail Description: The fun begins when you turn left off Buckhorn Road into a deep wash. This turn is very easy to miss, so follow directions carefully. A mostly rocky, sometimes sandy road climbs and descends a series of scenic mountain ridges with the steepest spot coming at 7.1 miles. Bradshaw's Grave is surrounded by a white picket fence and is hard to miss. Annie May White's Grave at Copperopolis Townsite is a short hike from the trail and takes a few minutes to find. Mining memorabilia has been removed from the UFO Mine as part of an extensive reclamation project.

Services: Full services in Wickenburg.

Directions: *(Shadowed portion of trail is described here.)*

WP	Mile	Action
01	0.0	*N34° 02.54´ W112° 36.77´* From start, bear right following Buckhorn Road.
	1.0	Bear left where Owl Springs Road goes right.
02	4.3	*N34° 02.91´ W112° 33.40´* IMPORTANT: Turn left off main road and drop steeply into wash. Look for corral and large rusty water tank hidden in trees. Climb rougher road to top of ridge and start down. Pass through gate and continue on winding, hilly road.
03	6.3	*N34° 03.94´ W112° 32.47´* Go straight up steep rocky hill where private road goes left at wash. Look for hidden mine ruins on hillside below on right. Locals say this is the site of historic Constellation City, but author could find no foundational remains to confirm.
	7.1	Descend steep, rocky ledge road, toughest part of trail. At bottom, enter sandy wash, prone to washouts.
	7.8	Pass through shade trees of Iron Spring.
04	8.0	*N34° 05.06´ W112° 31.87´* Make hard right uphill. Road climbs and descends Swallow Mountain.
05	10.0	*N 34° 05.61´ W 112° 30.74´* Continue straight. Road that joins on left goes to Crown Point Mine.
	10.6	Bear right at T intersection.
06	11.4	*N 34° 04.80´ W 112° 29.80´* Bear left at T intersection. (Easy to miss this turn on the return trip.)
07	11.7	*N 34° 04.86´ W 112° 29.64´* Trail continues right past Bradshaw's Grave on left.
	13.5	Pass through gate on rocky hillside. Road drops into wash and climbs steeply.
08	14.4	*N 34° 04.33´ W 112° 28.38´* Bear right downhill through gully. Road that joins on left goes to UFO Mine. When author was here in 2000, mine artifacts were scattered about. Apparently all were removed during mine reclamation.
	14.8	Bear left uphill at Y intersection. Road to right is difficult, dangerous Jeep road.
	15.7	Continue straight where a road goes right downhill. Just before this point, if you search the hillside below the trail, you'll find a 1939 grave of Annie May White.
09	15.9	*N 34° 04.80´ W 112° 27.89´* Low walls of stone cabin on right mark the general location of Copperopolis Townsite. Copperopolis Mine is across the ravine. Road continues short distance uphill to windmill and water tank.

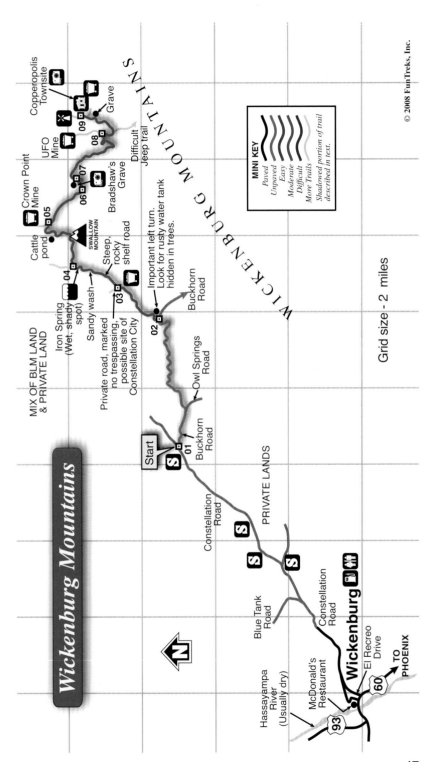

Wickenburg Mountains

WICKENBURG MOUNTAINS

MIX OF BLM LAND & PRIVATE LAND

Copperopolis Townsite

Grave

UFO Mine

Crown Point Mine

09

08

Bradshaw's Grave

07

06

05

Difficult Jeep trail

Cattle pond

SWALLOW MOUNTAIN

Steep, rocky shelf road

Iron Spring (Wet, shady spot)

04

Sandy wash

03

Private road, marked no trespassing, possible site of Constellation City

Important left turn. Look for rusty water tank hidden in trees.

02

Buckhorn Road

Owl Springs Road

Start

01

Buckhorn Road

Constellation Road

PRIVATE LANDS

Blue Tank Road

Constellation Road

Wickenburg

El Recreo Drive

60

TO PHOENIX

Hassayampa River (Usually dry)

McDonald's Restaurant

93

N

MINI KEY

Paved
Unpaved
Easy
Moderate
Difficult
More Trails

Shadowed portion of trail described in text.

© 2008 FunTreks, Inc.

Grid size - 2 miles

Banked turns make this trail fun for everyone.

Entrance to kids' practice area.

Boulders Off-Highway Vehicle Staging and Camping Area Rules

1. Riding limited to trail access.
2. No spin turns / donuts.
3. No dust.
4. Speed limit 15 m.p.h.
5. Respect others.
6. Pack out trash (43 CFR 8365.1-1).
7. Do not harass or disturb wildlife.
8. No shooting within 1/4 mile (43 CFR 8365.2-5).
9. Bring your own firewood, no pallets (43 CFR 8365.1-6).
10. All OHVs must be equipped with an approved spark arrester (43 CFR 8343).

Trail is mildly steep in places.   Rules are clearly posted. Read and follow.

Usually empty staging area during the week. Fills up on weekends, especially holidays.

Getting There: From Phoenix, head north on Interstate 17 to Carefree Exit 223. Drive west on Highway 74 about 18.6 miles. Turn right on dirt road 0.4 miles after mile marker 12. Follow LP6 north about a mile to staging area.

Staging/Camping: Staging area is very large and well defined. It includes modern vault toilet, small picnic area, children's practice area and room to camp. Plenty of space for large RVs and motorhomes. A great place to spend a weekend. Can get crowded on holiday weekends.

Difficulty: The route is relatively easy; however, intermittent steep spots require caution for novice riders. Adults should take their kids around the loop to be sure it is not too difficult for them. If the trail is too long for the little ones, they can shorten the trip by returning to staging area at various points along the way. Although the trail remains relatively close to the staging area, it is possible to make a wrong turn and head off in the wrong direction. Before you let your kids go alone, make sure they recognize all the turns and know which way to go. There is a vast desert area in which they could get lost, and it could be very dangerous, especially if they have no water.

Highlights: A step up in difficulty from the kids' practice area. This 4-mile loop offers lots of twists, turns and small hill climbs. Trail B winds back and forth in a narrow wash and is great fun. Adults will enjoy the trip as well. Go around several times or try it in the opposite direction to add variety.

Time & Distance: Complete 4-mile loop takes between 30 minutes and an hour depending on riding skills. Shorten the trip anytime by taking one of several shortcuts back to staging area.

Trail Description: Trail A is fairly straight but undulates up and down. Trail B is fairly flat but winds back and forth in a narrow wash. Both are fun. Once you've mastered this loop, you can explore many other trails beyond, including difficult Trail #6, described next.

Services: Full services near Carefree, Exit 223, east of Interstate 17. Modern vault toilet and a few picnic tables at staging area.

Directions: *(Shadowed portion of trail is described here.)*

WP	Mile	Action
01	**0.0**	*N33° 50.67´ W112° 26.54´* From toilet at staging area, head northwest on the main road LP6.
02	**0.3**	*N33° 50.90´ W112° 26.79´* Turn hard left on Trail A and head due south.
	0.5	Descend to bottom of small ravine and climb out again. Novice riders may find this spot a bit steep.
03	**0.9**	*N33° 50.42´ W112° 26.81´* Turn hard left staying on Trail A. Right here goes to Picacho Road with fast-moving trucks.
	1.2	Continue straight. (Trail D goes left back to staging area.)
	1.4	Continue straight and cross over LP6. Watch for cars.
	1.5	Continue straight. (Trail C goes left back to staging area.)
04	**1.5+**	*N33° 50.40´ W112° 26.22´* Just a short distance past Trail C, drop to bottom of ravine and turn left on Trail B.
05	**2.2**	*N33° 50.86´ W112° 26.58´* Continue straight in narrow wash on Trail B. Left is shortcut back to staging area.
06	**2.4**	*N33° 50.95´ W112° 26.80´* Continue straight on Trail B in narrow ravine. (Trail A crosses on a diagonal and climbs out of ravine on right.)
07	**3.0**	*N33° 51.28´ W112° 27.08´* Trail B ends at LP8 at T intersection. Turn left.
08	**3.1**	*N33° 51.27´ W112° 27.16´* Turn left on wider LP6 and head south back to staging area.
01	**4.0**	Return to toilet at staging area where you started.

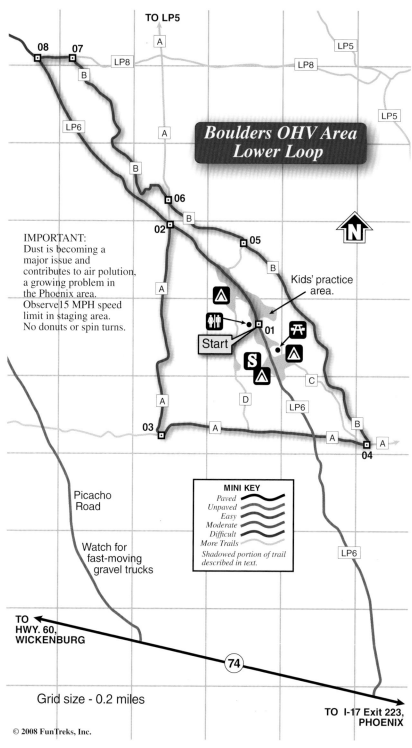

TO LP5

08 07

LP8

B

LP6

B

06

02 B

Boulders OHV Area Lower Loop

N

05

B

Kids' practice area.

IMPORTANT:
Dust is becoming a
major issue and
contributes to air polution,
a growing problem in
the Phoenix area.
Observe 15 MPH speed
limit in staging area.
No donuts or spin turns.

A

01

Start

S

C

A

D

LP6

A

B

03 A 04

Picacho
Road

Watch for
fast-moving
gravel trucks

MINI KEY
Paved
Unpaved
Easy
Moderate
Difficult
More Trails
*Shadowed portion of trail
described in text.*

LP6

**TO
HWY. 60,
WICKENBURG**

74

Grid size - 0.2 miles

**TO I-17 Exit 223,
PHOENIX**

© 2008 FunTreks, Inc.

Vault toilet at staging area.

Plenty of room for large campers.

Very steep in places. Not for beginners.

Like riding a giant roller coaster.

A few narrow, rocky spots in washes.

Trail climbs high enough to see all the way to Lake Pleasant.

52

Boulders OHV Area, Upper Lp. ⑥

Getting There: From Phoenix, head north on Interstate 17 to Carefree, Exit 223. Drive west on Highway 74 about 18.6 miles. Turn right on dirt road 0.4 miles after mile marker 12. Follow LP6 north about a mile to staging area.

Staging/Camping: Staging area is very large and well defined. It includes modern vault toilet, small picnic area, children's practice area and room to camp. Plenty of space for large RVs and motorhomes. A great place to spend a weekend.

Difficulty: South end is easy to moderate; however, as you proceed north, hills get very steep and difficult. For advanced riders only with 4-wheel-drive ATVs. Too much throttle on some hills could result in a dangerous backflip. A couple of challenging rocky sections. Trails are generally well marked, but there are so many, it is very easy to get lost. Don't let children ride off alone. One wrong turn and they could end up miles away. *Most routes in the area are wide enough for UTVs, but the exact route described here may be too steep for UTVs at the north end.*

Highlights: A giant, natural roller-coaster park at the north end. Many additional miles of steep, narrow, twisting trails to explore. Washes are generally easy, but have a few rocky sections. The final wash, heading west toward Picacho Road, has one challenging spot.

Time & Distance: Basic loop described here is about 13 miles and takes 3 to 4 hours. However, if you explore all the roads in the area, it could take several days.

Trail Description: Trail heads north, meandering in and out of sandy washes on the south end, then begins a gradual climb into the Hieroglyphic Mountains. Trails begin branching in all directions as hills get steeper and steeper. High points have incredible views in all directions with roads as far as the eye can see. You can continue north to the edge of the Hell's Canyon Wilderness. To avoid having to return over the same route, this trip follows an interesting wash west and connects to a wide gravel-hauling road. Watch for large speeding trucks along this busy road.

Services: Full services near Carefree, Exit 223, east of Interstate 17. Modern vault toilet and a few picnic tables at staging area.

53

Directions: *(Shadowed portion of trail is described here.)*

WP	Mile	Action
01	0.0	*N33° 50.67′ W112° 26.54′* From toilet at staging area, head northwest on the main road LP6.
02	0.3	*N33° 50.90′ W112° 26.79′* Turn right on Trail A and head due north. Make no turns as various trails cross at 0.4, 0.8 and 1.3 miles.
03	1.4	*N33° 51.81′ W112° 26.87′* Drop into a wide wash (LP5). Cross wash to other side bearing slightly right and continue on Trail A.
	1.5	Trail A ends. Continue northwest in wide wash LP5.
04	2.6	*N33° 52.68′ W112° 27.37′* Climb over steep, rocky ledge and bear right out of wash. Note windmill on left once out of wash. Continue northeast following signs for LP9.
05	4.2	*N33° 53.63′ W112° 26.83′* Turn right uphill on lesser trail and leave LP9.
	4.8	Stay left, then left again at 4.9. Right is an interesting side loop but has an extremely steep climb.
	5.2	Climb steep hill to top of ridge and turn left on LP11.
06	5.3	*N33° 54.08′ W112° 26.21′* LP9 goes downhill to left. (You'll come back here soon.) For now, continue straight uphill on LP11.
	5.4	Turn right downhill on narrow, rocky trail.
	5.7	At bottom of hill, turn right on LP10. Go past mine.
	6.0	Turn right at ridge LP11 and go back to Waypoint 06.
06	6.3	Turn left steeply downhill on LP9.
	7.2	Stay left and continue downhill on LP9 into wash.
07	7.6	*N33° 53.74′ W112° 26.94′* LP9 makes a steep uphill to left back to Wpt. 05. This way would take you back the way you came. Instead, for a different trip, bear right and stay in wash. Ignore next road uphill to right.
	8.7	Wash narrows at challenging boulder field. Bypass to left with "W" sign is illegal bypass to boulders.
	9.1	Bear right out of wash and pass through gate.
08	9.2	*N33° 53.39′ W112° 27.93′* Turn left on wide Picacho Road. Watch for speeding trucks from gravel pit.
09	10.3	*N33° 52.50′ W112° 27.69′* Turn left off Picacho Road onto LP6. Follow it south, ignoring side roads.
01	12.9	Return to staging area at toilet.

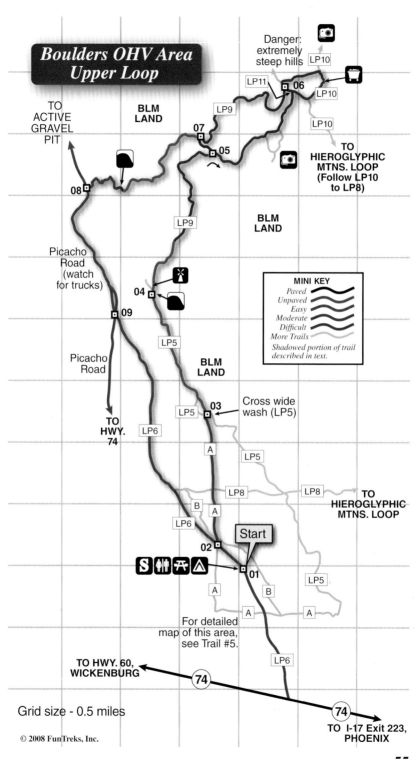

Boulders OHV Area Upper Loop

Danger: extremely steep hills

LP10

TO ACTIVE GRAVEL PIT

BLM LAND

LP11 06

LP9

LP10

LP10

07

05

LP10

TO HIEROGLYPHIC MTNS. LOOP (Follow LP10 to LP8)

08

BLM LAND

LP9

Picacho Road (watch for trucks)

04

MINI KEY
Paved
Unpaved
Easy
Moderate
Difficult
More Trails
Shadowed portion of trail described in text.

09

LP5

BLM LAND

Picacho Road

LP5   03   Cross wide wash (LP5)

TO HWY. 74

LP6

A

LP5

LP8   LP8   TO HIEROGLYPHIC MTNS. LOOP

B   A

LP6

Start

02

S ♦ ☷ ⛺   01

A   B

LP5

A   A

For detailed map of this area, see Trail #5.

LP6

TO HWY. 60, WICKENBURG   (74)

(74)

TO I-17 Exit 223, PHOENIX

Grid size - 0.5 miles

© 2008 FunTreks, Inc.

55

Painted "CK" rock at Waypoint 03.

Kiosk at Bradford Foothills staging area.

UTV on easy southern portion of route.

Skill needed to get over this ledge.

Last mile is rough but fun.

Prescott National Forest Road 192 begins its climb towards Crown King.

Side trip to Tunnel Mine.

Crown King General Store ends this trip.

Backway to Crown King ⑦

Getting There: From Phoenix, head north on Interstate 17 to Carefree, Exit 223. Drive west on Highway 74 about 11.4 miles and turn right on paved Castle Hot Springs Road just past mile marker 19. Continue north 5.5 miles and bear left (right goes to north end of Lake Pleasant). Pavement soon ends. Go another 3 miles and bear right on Cow Creek Road. Continue another 1.5 miles to staging area on right.

Staging/Camping: You are encouraged to park and camp in the main staging area on Cow Creek Road. Look for "Bradshaw Foothills" kiosk. This area is outside Lake Pleasant Regional Park and no fees are required (unless you ride into park). No facilities at staging area.

Difficulty: South end, prior to entering the Prescott National Forest, is maintained and is relatively easy. Conditions deteriorate as you head north with optional challenges available. Ledges increase in size before Oro Belle Mine, where a nasty boulder field begins the most difficult part of the trip. Four-wheel drive is required and riders should be advanced. The Crown King fire in 2008 may make the trail more difficult. *UTVs should be able to reach the Oro Belle Mine, but after that, most people on UTVs turn around.*

Highlights: Historic route passes numerous mine structures, many of which are hidden in dense trees. The tiny mountain town of Crown King is a popular tourist destination. Unlicensed ATVs risk a ticket on F.S. 52 and Crown King Road.

Time & Distance: Entire round trip described here is almost 50 miles. More than half is fast, easy riding, but the hard sections take time. Allow a full day for this adventure.

Trail Description: A long ride to point on trail where the action begins, but it's worth it. Final 4 miles climbs rapidly through dense forest with many challenges. A very historical area with great scenery. History buffs should read *Crown King and the Southern Bradshaws: A Complete History,* by Bruce M. Wilson.

Services: No services enroute. Crown King General Store has gas. (See appendix for phone number.)

Directions: *(Shadowed portion of trail is described here.)*

WP	Mile	Action
01	**0.0**	*N33° 57.05´ W112° 18.79´* From main staging, head north on Cow Creek Road.
02	**5.8**	*N34° 01.18´ W112° 20.25´* Stay right and continue north on Cow Creek Road where Champie Road joins on left.
03	**9.7** **Reset**	*N34° 03.64´ W112° 21.94´* Turn right at large rock with painted letters "CK" (see photo). Head north on easy road across private land. Road gradually gets rougher and steeper.
	5.8	Boundary to Prescott National Forest. Road becomes F.S. 711.
	6.7	Camp spots on left at historic site of Fort Misery. Look for remains of stone cabin.
	6.9	Difficult washed-out spot. More obstacles follow.
04	**9.8**	*N34° 10.35´ W112° 21.66´* Make hard right up steep switchback. Trail becomes F.S. 192.
05	**10.6**	*N34° 10.24´ W112° 20.92´* Remains of Oro Belle Mine on right after difficult rocky ledge.
	10.7	Turn hard left downhill, then climb though difficult rocky boulder field. Road continues uphill on steep, narrow shelf road.
	11.8	Stay right on main trail. Narrow road to left goes to buildings at Tunnel Mine (see photo).
	12.7	Road is not as steep, but boulders increase in size. Trail is challenging and fun to ride.
	13.2	Stay right at "Y." Boulders continue.
06	**13.7**	*N34° 11.89´ W112° 21.19´* Turn right at "T" intersection at larger F.S. 52, called Senator Highway. (ATVs should have "MC" license plate on this road.)
	14.8	Turn left at major "T" intersection. F.S. 259 goes right to Horsethief Basin Recreation Area.
07	**15.5**	*N34° 12.34´ W112° 20.26´* Turn left into tiny town of Crown King. Make sure to stop at the Crown King General Store for some of their great homemade fudge.
01	**40.7**	Return the way you came to staging area on Cow Creek Road.

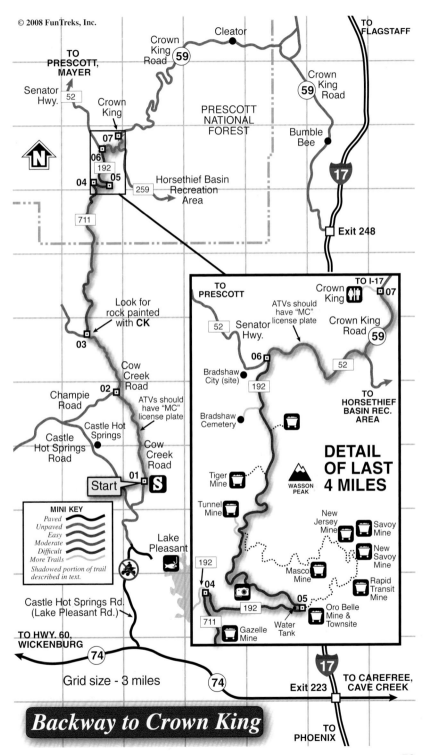

© 2008 FunTreks, Inc.

TO FLAGSTAFF

Cleator

Crown King Road **59**

TO PRESCOTT, MAYER

Crown King Road **59**

Senator Hwy. **52**

Crown King

07

06

192

05

04

259

711

N

PRESCOTT NATIONAL FOREST

Bumble Bee

17

Horsethief Basin Recreation Area

Exit 248

Look for rock painted with **CK**

03

Cow Creek Road

02

Champie Road

Castle Hot Springs

ATVs should have "MC" license plate

Castle Hot Springs Road

Cow Creek Road

Start **01** **S**

MINI KEY
Paved
Unpaved
Easy
Moderate
Difficult
More Trails
Shadowed portion of trail described in text.

Lake Pleasant

Castle Hot Springs Rd. (Lake Pleasant Rd.)

TO HWY. 60, WICKENBURG

74

Grid size - 3 miles

74

DETAIL OF LAST 4 MILES

TO PRESCOTT

TO I-17

Crown King

07

ATVs should have "MC" license plate

Crown King Road **59**

Senator Hwy. **52**

06

52

TO HORSETHIEF BASIN REC. AREA

Bradshaw City (site)

192

Bradshaw Cemetery

WASSON PEAK

Tiger Mine

Tunnel Mine

New Jersey Mine

Savoy Mine

New Savoy Mine

Masson Mine

192

04

192

711

Gazelle Mine

Water Tank

05

Oro Belle Mine & Townsite

Rapid Transit Mine

17

Exit 223

TO CAREFREE, CAVE CREEK

TO PHOENIX

Backway to Crown King

59

Walk a short distance to see Tule Creek Homestead. Watch for rattlesnakes.

Trail heads north into mountains.

Optional side trip to mine from Waypoint 06.

Reaching east side of this optional side canyon requires passing through difficult spot.

Tule Creek Homestead 8

Getting There: From Phoenix, head north on Interstate 17 to Carefree, Exit 223. Drive west on Highway 74 about 11.4 miles and turn right on paved Castle Hot Springs Road just past mile marker 19. Continue north 5.5 miles and bear left (right goes to north end of Lake Pleasant). Pavement soon ends. Go another 3 miles and bear right on Cow Creek Road. Continue another 1.5 miles to staging area on right.

Staging/Camping: You are encouraged to park and camp in the main staging area on Cow Creek Road. Look for the "Bradshaw Foothills" kiosk. This area is outside Lake Pleasant Regional Park and no fees are required (unless you ride into park). No facilities at staging area.

Difficulty: Main trail is mostly easy with a few moderate rocky sections. Side trips have difficult spots, especially the east side of canyon pictured on bottom of opposite page.

Highlights: Much remains of the main building at the Tule Creek Homestead (our name for it, not its official name), due to its sturdy concrete and metal construction. It's a fun place to explore—just watch for rattlesnakes. Please leave everything as you find it.

Time & Distance: Entire trip described here is 16.6 miles. More than half is fast, easy riding. Allow 2 to 3 hours plus additional time for optional side trips.

Trail Description: Main trail climbs gradually into the foothills of the Bradshaw Mountains to the border of Tule Creek Riparian Management Area. From here, it is a short walk to a photogenic homestead. It's a pleasant ride with high views of Lake Pleasant, but otherwise fairly uneventful. If you can handle more difficulty, consider adding three side trips that add much interest. The first is a deep canyon south of Waypoint 04. A moderate trip down the west side of the canyon is fairly short but very scenic. A trip down the east side is longer and very dramatic (see photo at left), however it requires passing through a difficult, narrow, tippy spot. A third side trip departs east from Waypoint 07. A series of narrow trails split several times, one of which leads to a large vertical mine shaft.

Services: Gas at I-17, Exit 223. Camping at staging area, but no toilets.

Directions: *(Shadowed portion of trail is described here.)*

WP	Mile	Action
01	**0.0**	*N33° 57.05´ W112° 18.79´* Head north from staging area on Cow Creek Road.
02	**1.1**	*N33° 57.92´ W112° 18.73´* Bear right off Cow Creek Road. Road climbs or goes around steep hill.
	1.5	Bear left.
03	**2.0.**	*N33° 58.57´ W112° 18.57´* Bear right.
	2.2	Bear right as you slowly descend a hill.
	3.3	Use caution; hill gets steeper. Easiest route will be on left side.
	3.4	Turn left to reach water crossing. (Optional: Right goes south along west side of canyon.)
04	**3.5**	*N33° 58.01´ W112° 17.60´* After water crossing, turn left at T to continue on main trail. (Optional: Right goes south along east side of canyon, but entry point is difficult.)
05	**4.0**	*N33° 58.40´ W112° 17.44´* Continue straight. (Road on right is exit point of loop. You'll return here later)
	5.7	Continue straight as road joins from right. (This is start of loop for return trip.)
06	**5.9**	*N33° 59.80´ W112° 16.88´* Bear right. Trail gets a little rougher.
07	**7.1**	*N34° 00.11´ W112° 15.99´* Bear left at major intersection and pass through gate. (Right is optional and more difficult side trip to mine.)
08	**7.6**	*N34° 00.30´ W112° 16.27´* Trail ends at permanently closed gate. Take short walk to homestead, then return to Waypoint 06.
06	**9.3**	Bear left.
	9.5	Bear left and begin different loop back.
	10.9	Bear right uphill on lesser road.
09	**11.1**	*N33° 58.45´ W112° 16.31´* Bear right and follow steep trail back to main trail.
05	**12.6**	Return to main trail. Turn left and go out the way you came in. (Consider exploring optional scenic canyon mentioned earlier.)

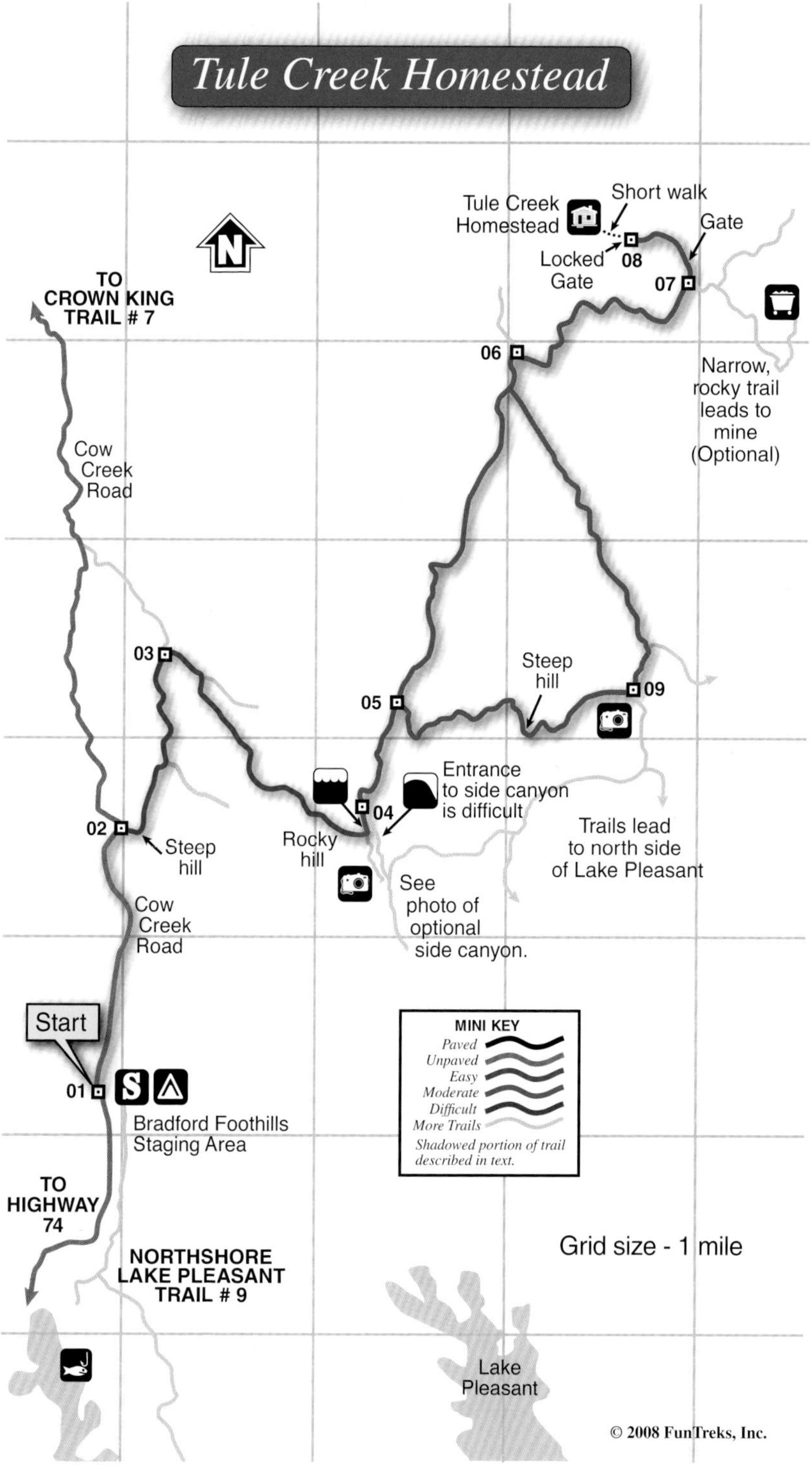

Tule Creek Homestead

N

Tule Creek Homestead

Short walk

Locked Gate

Gate

08

07

TO
CROWN KING
TRAIL # 7

Narrow,
rocky trail
leads to
mine
(Optional)

Cow
Creek
Road

06

03

Steep
hill

05

09

Entrance
to side canyon
is difficult

Trails lead
to north side
of Lake Pleasant

02

Steep
hill

Rocky
hill

04

Cow
Creek
Road

See
photo of
optional
side canyon.

Start

MINI KEY

Paved
Unpaved
Easy
Moderate
Difficult
More Trails
*Shadowed portion of trail
described in text.*

01

S **⌂**

Bradford Foothills
Staging Area

TO
HIGHWAY
74

Grid size - 1 mile

**NORTHSHORE
LAKE PLEASANT
TRAIL # 9**

Lake
Pleasant

© 2008 FunTreks, Inc.

A few easy hills.

Numerous coves to explore.

Local fisherman enjoys a relaxing afternoon.

Cove west of Waypoint 04.

Road heads south to Waypoint 06.

Northshore Lake Pleasant

Getting There: From Phoenix, head north on Interstate 17 to Carefree, Exit 223. Drive west on Highway 74 about 11.4 miles and turn right on paved Castle Hot Springs Road just past mile marker 19. Continue north 5.5 miles and bear left. (Right goes to Lake Pleasant. There's a self-pay fee station here, where you can get a park pass.) Pavement soon ends. Go another 3 miles and bear right on Cow Creek Road. Continue another 1.5 miles to staging area on right.

Staging/Camping: You are encouraged to park and camp in the main staging area on Cow Creek Road. Look for the "Bradshaw Foothills" kiosk. This area is outside Lake Pleasant Regional Park and no fees are required to park; however, since you will be riding into the park, you'll need a pass. Camping is allowed around the lake, but please pack out your trash. Whenever possible, carry out trash left by others. Bring your own firewood and pack out your ashes.

Difficulty: Easy. Main trail is wide and smooth with gradual hills. Great route for new riders. Route is mostly hard packed dirt and is dusty.

Highlights: Trail provides easy access to beautiful coves along north shore of Lake Pleasant. Area is small, but it takes a while to cover if you explore all the coves. Great for weekend campouts. You'll need a fishing license if you fish.

Time & Distance: Trip described here is 9.4 miles. Allow a couple of hours plus additional time to explore coves.

Trail Description: You'll head south from staging area into Lake Pleasant Regional Park (pass required). Trail has two main forks with countless secondary forks. All lead to water's edge or viewpoints along cliffs. Some trails lead into the water and continue farther when lake is low. Never enter the water on your ATV; this could pollute the lake. Water levels are usually high from February through May, then decrease to lowest levels August through October. Staging area for this trail is same as for Trails 7 and 8. Take a long weekend and explore all three trails. More trails east of staging area.

Services: Gas at I-17, Exit 223. Camping at staging area, but no toilets.

Directions: *(Shadowed portion of trail is described here.)*

WP	Mile	Action
01	**0.0**	*N33° 57.05´ W112° 18.79´* Head south from kiosk at staging area. Trail runs along side of Cow Creek Road and is identified with brown trail markers.
	0.6	Continue straight. (Optional trails go east away from coves.)
02	**1.1**	*N33° 56.14´ W112° 18.90´* Bear left.
03	**1.9**	*N33° 55.57´ W112° 18.45´* Bear right at major fork. You will come back to this point later.
	2.1	Bear left.
	2.2	Bear left.
04	**2.4**	*N33° 55.24´ W112° 18.40´* Turn right and ride to beautiful cove with high cliffs (see picture). Return to Waypoint 04 and turn right.
	3.0	Bear left. Right goes to end of peninsula with another scenic view.
	3.3	Bear left.
05	**3.4**	*N33° 54.85´ W112° 18.19´* Bear right. Follow road to end of cove with sandy shore (see picture of fisherman). Return to Waypoint 03.
03	**4.6** **Reset**	*N33° 55.57´ W112° 18.45´* Bear right heading southeast.
	0.8	First trail goes to left. Stay right until you reach Waypoint 06.
06	**1.3**	*N33° 54.92´ W112° 17.56´* Bear right and ride to water's edge.
	1.4	Trail ends. (Based on water level in late May. In the fall, when water level is lower, trail may go farther.)
	2.8	Explore other coves on this peninsula, then return the way you came, heading north at Waypoint 03.

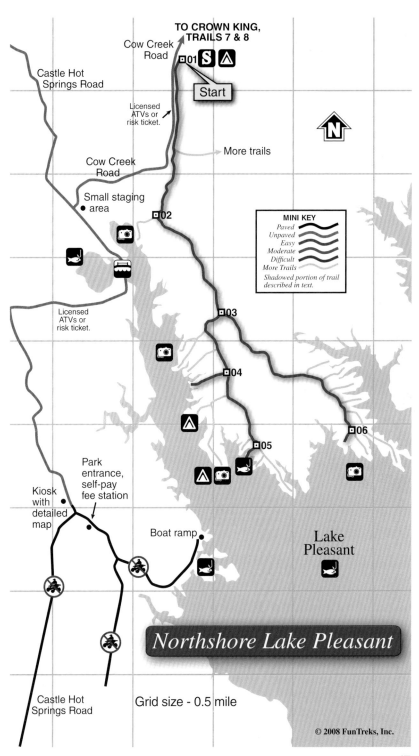

TO CROWN KING,
TRAILS 7 & 8

Cow Creek Road

01 S A

Start

Castle Hot Springs Road

Licensed ATVs or risk ticket.

More trails

Cow Creek Road

Small staging area

02

MINI KEY
Paved
Unpaved
Easy
Moderate
Difficult
More Trails
Shadowed portion of trail described in text.

Licensed ATVs or risk ticket.

03

04

05

06

Park entrance, self-pay fee station

Kiosk with detailed map

Boat ramp

Lake Pleasant

Northshore Lake Pleasant

Castle Hot Springs Road

Grid size - 0.5 mile

© 2008 FunTreks, Inc.

Tippy spot at Waypoint 04.

Rocky and steep after mine.

Great view at high point of trail.

Waypoint 06. Author stopped here.

Cleator Bar, a popular stop after a long, hot day of riding. (Open weekends only.)

Getting There: From Phoenix, head north on Interstate 17 to Bumble Bee Exit 248. Follow Crown King Road north about 15 miles to Cleator. Continue another 1.2 miles to F.S. 259B on right. A quicker, but less scenic route is to go farther north on I-17 to Exit 259. Head west to Cordes and turn left on Antelope Creek Road. Head south to Crown King Road and turn right towards Cleator. (Note: A controversial plan to reroute I-17 through Bumble Bee could affect roads in area.)

Staging/Camping: Staging area is located on the south side of Crown King Road opposite start of trail at F.S. 259B. Not an ideal camping spot. A popular place to camp is south of Bumble Bee on Castle Creek Road, F.S. 684. ATVs are allowed on Crown King Road, but should have an "MC" license plate (see page 14).

Difficulty: Moderate before the mine. After that, it gets very steep and tippy in places. Even advanced riders will take pause at key points along the route. The first tippy spot, shown in top left photo, doesn't accurately depict how tippy it is. There are no trees or rocks around to attach a winch line and footing is poor. Should you roll your ATV, it's a long way to the bottom of the hill. Travel with other experienced riders to assist one another. Author turned around at Waypoint 06 and does not recommend this trail for ATVs beyond this point. *Not recommended for UTVs after Waypoint 03.*

Highlights: A high-elevation trail with great views, but what you'll remember most about this trail is its tippy spots and steep climbs. The trails that pass through Desoto Mine are on private land. F.S. 259B stops at the property line. Warning signs stress the dangers of entering.

Time & Distance: Round trip is just 12.8 miles as described here. Allow 3 to 4 hours. With the long drive to start of trail, plan an entire day for this adventure. Consider combining with Dead Cow Gulch, Trail #11.

Trail Description: Ride to mine is relaxing, fun and scenic. After the mine, conditions become borderline dangerous. Don't hesitate to turn around if conditions are beyond your skill level.

Services: Cleator has a general store and bar, which is very popular on weekends (only time it's open). Stop in and chat with the locals, who may be able to tell you more about the area.

Directions: *(Shadowed portion of trail is described here.)*

WP	Mile	Action
01	0.0	*N34° 16.63´ W112° 15.21´* From staging area on south side of Crown King Road, cross road and head north on F.S. 259B.
	0.4	Stay right past county gravel pit. Road gets rougher as it climbs long hill.
02	1.5	*N34° 17.37´ W112° 15.70´* At top of hill, pass through gate and close it.
	2.6	Stay right past corral and continue to climb.
03	3.2	*N34° 17.15´ W112° 17.02´* Large brown metal water tank on left. Turn right on F.S. 9268R to go around Desoto Mine, private property. (F.S. 259B continues straight and runs into property line. A dirt barricade has not prevented people from continuing through the mine.)
	3.7	Stay left where 9210A goes right.
04	3.8	*N34° 17.59´ W112° 16.89´* Dangerous tippy spot. All riders use extreme caution. Turn around if not 100% confident. Recommend using spotter or safety strap. If your ATV rolls here, it's a long way to the bottom of hill.
05	4.5 *Reset*	*N34° 17.65´ W112° 17.42´* Driver's choice. A narrow, rutted, steep road to left climbs to a high point above Desoto Mine. The road makes a loop and circles back down. This side trip adds 1.8 miles. Right at Waypoint 05 continues on an increasingly steep and tippy trail. For advanced riders, only.
06	1.0	*N34° 17.91´ W112° 18.29´* Extremely steep, rocky hill. Author chose to turn around. Road continues and runs into F.S. 89, which connects to Senator Highway, F.S. 52.
01	6.5	Return to staging area.

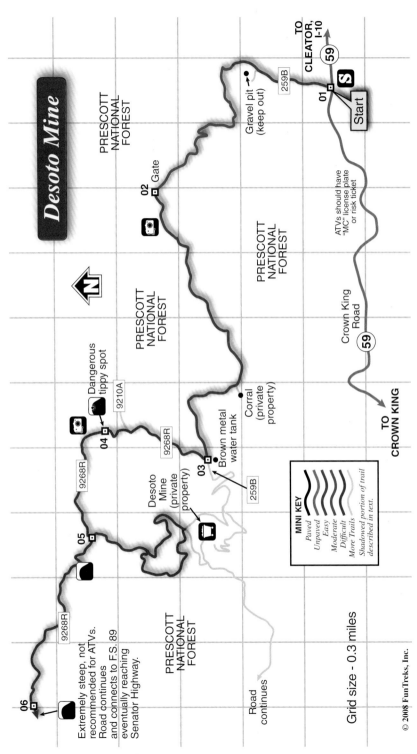

Desoto Mine

PRESCOTT NATIONAL FOREST

TO CLEATOR, I-10

59

S

Start

01

259B

Gravel pit (keep out)

ATVs should have "MC" license plate or risk ticket

02 Gate

PRESCOTT NATIONAL FOREST

PRESCOTT NATIONAL FOREST

N

Crown King Road

59

TO CROWN KING

Dangerous tippy spot

9210A

04

9268R

Desoto Mine (private property)

Corral (private property)

Brown metal water tank

03

259B

9268R

05

9268R

06

Extremely steep, not recommended for ATVs. Road continues and connects to F.S. 89 eventually reaching Senator Highway.

PRESCOTT NATIONAL FOREST

Road continues

MINI KEY
Paved
Unpaved
Easy
Moderate
Difficult
More Trails
Shadowed portion of trail described in text.

Grid size - 0.3 miles

© 2008 FunTreks, Inc.

One of several historic buildings at Bumble Bee could be lost to freeway rerouting.

Narrow spot for Jeeps. OK for ATVs.

Trail crosses rocky creek several times.   Howard Copper Mine. Unsafe to enter.

Take a picnic lunch and enjoy the great scenery.

Dead Cow Gulch 11

Getting There: From Phoenix, head north on Interstate 17 to Bumble Bee, Exit 248. Follow Crown King Road, C.R. 59, west a couple of miles, then continue north after pavement ends. Continue another 3 miles and watch for Castle Creek Road, F.S. 684, on the left. (This road is not well marked.) Turn left on 684 and go short distance to staging and camping on right. Return to C.R. 59 to start ride. (Note: A controversial plan to reroute I-17 could change roads in the area.)

Staging/Camping: Staging area extends a considerable distance along 684 and will accommodate large groups for parking and camping. No toilets or trash receptacles. Pack out everything. Trip loops back to staging area. Crown King Road allows ATVs, but you should have an "MC" license plate (see page 14). If your ATV has an "RV" plate, have someone drop you off at Waypoint 02 or ride trail in both directions, without going on Crown King Road.

Difficulty: Fairly rocky along the creek beds, but no major obstacles. A narrow ledge at Waypoint 05 is a challenge for Jeeps, but is plenty wide enough for ATVs. (Author's note: We drove this trail in a Jeep, but saw nothing that would be a problem for ATVs.)

Highlights: A fun trail to ride with a variety of terrain. On a hot day, cool off in clear-water pools along the creeks. As you ride north, you'll pass through historic Bumble Bee (if new freeway doesn't wipe out the town). Before you head south on F.S. 9223C, consider going another mile on Crown King Road to Cleator, where you'll find local color and a popular weekend bar. Dead Cow Gulch is remote and lightly traveled; don't count on help if you have a breakdown.

Time & Distance: Entire loop measures 19.8 miles. More than 9 miles is fast-moving graded road. Allow 5 to 6 hours.

Trail Description: After a quick trip north along Crown King Road, you'll head south through Prescott National Forest and enter drainage for Black Canyon and Dead Cow Gulch. Much of trail winds back and forth across rocky creek beds. Final third of trip climbs into foothills and ends with scenic descent to Castle Creek Road. Interesting Howard Copper Mine is next to trail. Do not enter mines.

Services: Weekend bar and general store at Cleator.

Directions: *(Shadowed portion of trail is described here.)*

WP	Mile	Action
01	**0.0**	*N34° 11.33´ W112° 09.85´* Head north on Crown King Road from Castle Creek Road, F.S. 684.
	1.1	Pass through historic Bumble Bee, then stay left at next 3 intersections, following signs to Crown King.
02	**9.4** **Reset**	*N34° 16.49´ W112° 13.12´* Turn left on F.S. 9223C. This point is 1.1 miles after large concrete bridge. (Interesting town of Cleator is another mile on Crown King Road. Bar is open on weekends.)
	0.7	Stay right. (Left goes to Gray Goose Mine.)
	0.8	Continue straight.
03	**1.0**	*N34° 15.91´ W112° 13.50´* Turn left on F.S. 101.
	2.9	Bear left at Y intersection.
	3.3	First of many water crossings.
	3.7	Continue straight. (Left goes to active mine.)
04	**4.3**	*N34° 13.67´ W112° 12.66´* Bear left and begin following rocky creek. Ignore lesser side roads.
	5.0	Trail drops into creek. Turn hard left to avoid bad spot, then cross creek to right and continue south, weaving in and out of creek.
	5.9	Leave Prescott National Forest. Cattle guard marks boundary.
05	**6.1**	*N34° 12.91´ W112° 11.74´* Cross narrow, tippy ledge around rock wall. (Tough spot for Jeeps.)
	6.4	Stay left. Do not bear right uphill, yet.
	6.6	Turn hard right uphill on rocky road. (Note large opening to Howard Copper Mine on left.)
	7.5	Continue straight past Black Canyon horse trail. Pass through high area with scenic views.
06	**9.1**	*N34° 11.05´ W112° 10.61´* Bear left on larger Castle Creek Road 684 after creek crossing.
	9.8	Driver's choice.
	9.9	Bear left.
	10.3	Staging and camping area on left.
01	**10.4**	Intersect with Crown King Road where you started.

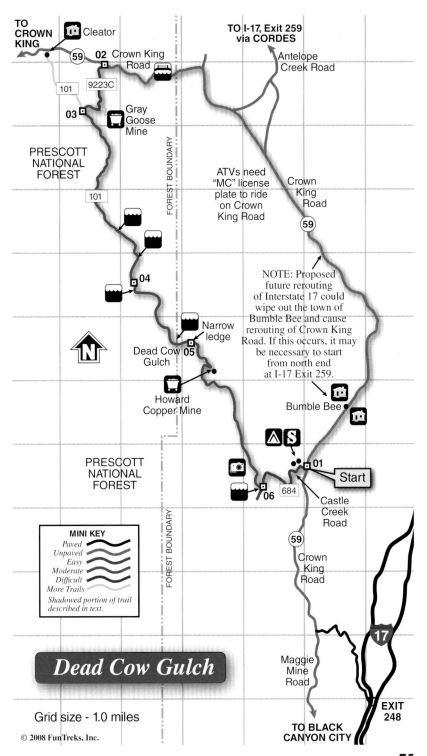

TO CROWN KING

Cleator

59 02 Crown King Road

TO I-17, Exit 259 via CORDES

Antelope Creek Road

101

9223C

03

Gray Goose Mine

PRESCOTT NATIONAL FOREST

FOREST BOUNDARY

101

ATVs need "MC" license plate to ride on Crown King Road

Crown King Road

59

04

NOTE: Proposed future rerouting of Interstate 17 could wipe out the town of Bumble Bee and cause rerouting of Crown King Road. If this occurs, it may be necessary to start from north end at I-17 Exit 259.

N

Narrow ledge

Dead Cow 05 Gulch

Howard Copper Mine

Bumble Bee

S

01

Start

PRESCOTT NATIONAL FOREST

FOREST BOUNDARY

06 684

Castle Creek Road

59

Crown King Road

MINI KEY
Paved
Unpaved
Easy
Moderate
Difficult
More Trails
Shadowed portion of trail described in text.

17

Dead Cow Gulch

Maggie Mine Road

EXIT 248

Grid size - 1.0 miles

© 2008 FunTreks, Inc.

TO BLACK CANYON CITY

Stay out of mines.

Descending into canyon.

Trail is fairly short, but fun to ride. Flash floods possible.

Shady spot for lunch break.

Remains of old mining cabin.

Several water crossings.

Black Canyon

Getting There: From Phoenix, head north on Interstate 17 to Exit 244, just north of Black Canyon City. Head west under freeway and connect to Maggie Mine Road, which goes west a short distance, then turns north. Watch for staging area on left in about 1.4 miles near end of pavement.

Staging/Camping: Small staging area has room for several vehicles, but no toilet or camping. Alternate staging area is less than a mile ahead on left, but again, there are no facilities.

Difficulty: Loop portion of trail drops moderately into Black Canyon. Trail weaves back and forth across bottom of canyon that is usually just a dry, sandy wash with occasional small rock challenges. Dangerous flash floods are always possible, so keep your eye on the sky. Most difficult part of trip begins at Waypoint 06, where you turn right out of canyon and begin steep rocky climb. This hill may be intimidating to novice riders.

Highlights: A short, fun ride with moderate challenges through historic mining country. According to our local guide, some mine adits can be hiked up to a mile into the mountain; however, javelina (wild pigs) sometimes inhabit the mines. Normally fearful of humans, javelina have been known to attack when their escape route is blocked. Other dangers include poison gas and cave-ins—these are three great reasons not to enter a mine that may look safe.

Time & Distance: Entire round trip from staging area and back is only 12.4 miles. Allow 2 to 3 hours. To extend your day, combine this trail with Dead Cow Gulch, Trail #11. It can be reached by taking Maggie Mine Road north and connecting to Crown King Road. (Author's note: If freeway is rerouted through Bumble Bee, roads north will change.)

Trail Description: Follow well-maintained gravel road north, then head west to backcountry loop which drops into Black Canyon. (Author's note: When we rode this trail, construction of a major pipeline through the area was almost complete. Everything should be back to normal by the time you read this.)

Services: You'll find restaurants, gas and basic services in Black Canyon City and Rock Springs between exits 242 and 244.

Directions: *(Shadowed portion of trail is described here.)*

WP	Mile	Action
01	**0.0**	*N34° 06.00´ W112° 08.85´* Head north on Maggie Mine Road from staging area where pavement ends.
	0.8	Alternate staging area on left.
	1.1	Slow down for residence on right to minimize dust. Road swings right uphill.
	2.0	Stay left on main road. (Lesser road to right climbs to high point near freeway.)
	3.0	Road swings right. Tiny road to left drops downhill to large mine adit (see photo).
02	**3.4** *Reset*	*N34° 07.70´ W112° 09.85´* Turn left off Maggie Mine Road onto trail.
03	**0.3**	*N 34° 07.77´ W112° 10.03´* Turn left to begin loop.
	0.7	Pass through old dilapidated cattle gate.
04	**1.2**	*N34° 07.36´ W112° 10.52´* Bear right at 3-way fork near old mining camp.
	1.2+	Make left into wash, then head west about a hundred feet and turn right up steep hill.
05	**1.5**	*N34° 07.52´ W112° 10.60´* Continue straight. (Left is a difficult Jeep trail called "Turkey Creek." It's an extremely difficult trail for ATVs.)
	1.6	Cross wash a couple of times, then follow faint trail along left side of wash.
	2.1	Bear left out of wash.
	2.5	After a couple of water crossings, difficult "Turkey Creek" Jeep trail rejoins on left.
	2.9	Low walls of old stone mining cabin on left.
06	**3.0**	*N34° 08.42´ W112° 10.58´* Make a hard right and climb steeply out of canyon. This spot may be intimidating to novice riders.
	3.2	Stay left.
03	**4.0**	Bear left and go out the way you came in.
02	**4.3**	Return to Maggie Mine Road. Turn right to return to start. (Left heads north and connects to Crown King Road towards Bumble Bee and Trails 10 and 11.)
01	**7.7**	Arrive back at staging area.

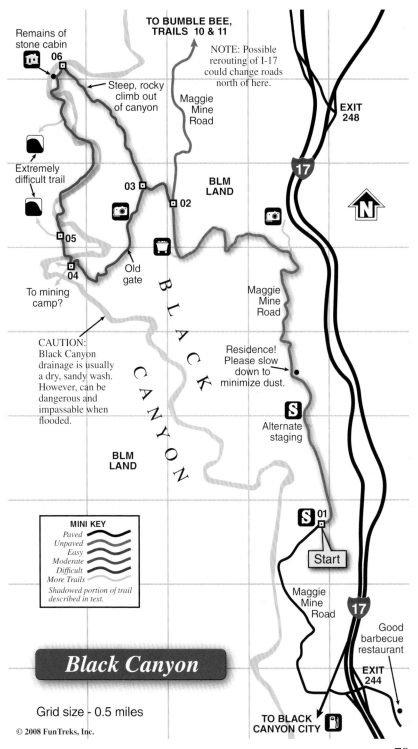

Remains of
stone cabin

06

Steep, rocky
climb out
of canyon

TO BUMBLE BEE,
TRAILS 10 & 11

NOTE: Possible
rerouting of I-17
could change roads
north of here.

Maggie
Mine
Road

EXIT
248

17

Extremely
difficult trail

03

02

BLM
LAND

05

Old
gate

04

To mining
camp?

CAUTION:
Black Canyon
drainage is usually
a dry, sandy wash.
However, can be
dangerous and
impassable when
flooded.

B
L
A
C
K

C
A
N
Y
O
N

Maggie
Mine
Road

Residence!
Please slow
down to
minimize dust.

N

S

Alternate
staging

BLM
LAND

MINI KEY

Paved
Unpaved
Easy
Moderate
Difficult
More Trails
Shadowed portion of trail
described in text.

S 01

Start

Maggie
Mine
Road

17

Good
barbecue
restaurant

EXIT
244

Black Canyon

Grid size - 0.5 miles

© 2008 FunTreks, Inc.

TO BLACK
CANYON CITY

Burfind Hotel at Gillette.

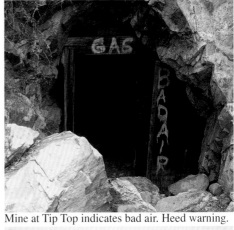

Agua Fria River usually not deep.

Mine at Tip Top indicates bad air. Heed warning.

Popular area for Hummer tours.

View from corner of Indian fort.

Long span of ruins at Tip Top Townsite. Mines are on hillsides above townsite.

Gillette Historic Tour

Getting There: From Phoenix, head north on Interstate 17 to Table Mesa Road, Exit 236. Cross over to west side of freeway and bear right on Table Mesa Road. Don't miss this turn or you'll get back on the freeway. Go north 0.6 miles and watch for large staging area on left.

Staging/Camping: Staging area is flat but has no toilets or other amenities. Pack out your trash. Most people come to this area to ride the vast network of roads available, not for the scenery, which, frankly, is not that great until you get into the hills west of Agua Fria River.

Difficulty: The route selected here is relatively easy and has been chosen primarily for its historical value; however, it is mildly rocky and steep in places. Parts of trail follow washes, which can change after heavy rains and flooding. Agua Fria River is usually shallow, but not always. Flash floods are always possible. Other roads in the area include several popular extreme Jeeping trails with names like Raw Deal, Terminator, Predator and Annihilator.

Highlights: See remains of the 1870s Burfind Hotel in the ghost town of Gillette. Gillette was the milling town for Tip Top Mine, which is the last stop on this trip. Patient explorers will find many hidden surprises at Tip Top, so take time and look around. After Gillette, make a stop at a hilltop Indian fort and enjoy great 360-degree views.

Time & Distance: One-way trip ending at Tip Top Mine measures 12.8 miles. Total time there and back is about 6 hours. Spend the rest of the day exploring other roads.

Trail Description: First part of trip is not that impressive as you ride along a wide, dusty, gravel road. Scenery improves after you cross the Agua Fria River and head east to Gillette. When you leave Gillette, for some extra fun and challenge, follow a side road north up a steep hill to a high overlook. This road reconnects to main route slighly north of Waypoint 02. Next stop is an Indian fort just one more mile up the main road. The final leg to Tip Top Mine is the longest and most remote part of the trip. As you climb into the higher hills after the fort, the road gets rougher, especially the last 2-1/2 miles, which follows a rocky, sandy wash.

Services: Closest gas is at New River, Exit 232, on Interstate 10.

Directions: *(Shadowed portion of trail is described here.)*

WP	Mile	Action
01	0.0	*N33° 58.57′ W112° 07.95′* Head north from staging area on wide Table Mesa Road. Stay right where roads branch left at 0.5, 1.0 and 1.7 miles.
	2.1	Stay left where lesser road goes right.
	2.6	Bear left, then cross wash at 2.7.
	3.7	Cross Agua Fria River (usually shallow).
02	4.0	*N34° 01.06′ W112° 09.98′* Turn hard right off main road to see Gillette. As you head east, ignore roads that go left uphill.
03	4.2	*N34° 01.13′ W112° 09.82′* Arrive at Gillette. All that remains are stone walls of Burfind Hotel. Return to Waypoint 02.
02	4.4 Reset	Bear right and continue north then west on main road.
04	1.0	*N34° 01.19′ W112° 10.76′* Bear left off main road then immediately bear right.
05	1.4	*N34° 00.97′ W112° 10.96′* Indian fort on right. Return to Waypoint 04.

WP	Mile	Action
04	1.8 Reset	Bear left and continue north and west on main road.
06	1.6	*N34° 02.08′ W112° 11.60′* Bear left before corral. Road climbs, then begins long descent.
07	4.2	*N34° 01.63′ W112° 13.60′* Bear right at bottom of hill in wash and begin following wash north. Road is rocky in places depending on conditions in wash.
	4.9	Pass through corral.
	6.4	Continue north past remains of building on right.
08	6.6	*N34° 03.04′ W112° 14.83′* Ruins on left identify townsite of Tip Top. More ruins and many mines on hillsides on both sides of road. (Main road continues another 2.2 miles past windmills and more mines. Private land at 2.2 miles is occupied. Stay out. Lesser road continues.)

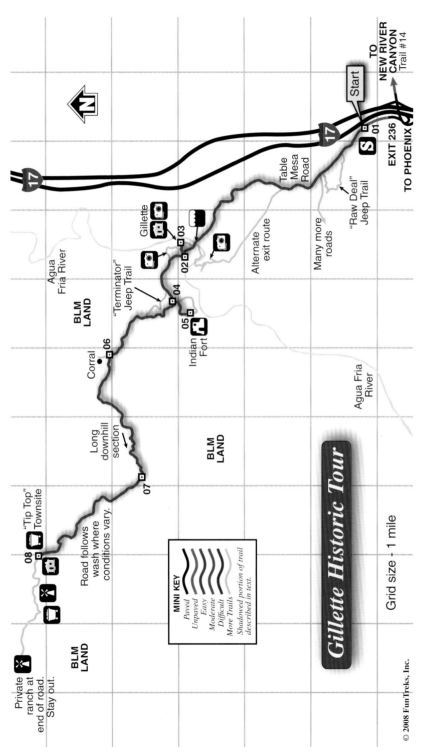

Gillette Historic Tour

Grid size - 1 mile

© 2008 FunTreks, Inc.

N

TO NEW RIVER CANYON Trail #14

Start

TO PHOENIX

EXIT 236

01

17

17

Table Mesa Road

"Raw Deal" Jeep Trail

Alternate exit route

Many more roads

Agua Fria River

Gillette

03

02

"Terminator" Jeep Trail

04

BLM LAND

05

Indian Fort

06

Corral

Agua Fria River

Long downhill section

BLM LAND

07

Road follows wash where conditions vary.

"Tip Top" Townsite

08

BLM LAND

Private ranch at end of road. Stay out.

MINI KEY
Paved
Unpaved
Easy
Moderate
Difficult
More Trails
Shadowed portion of trail described in text.

83

Bear left through this gate.

Road leads into Tonto National Forest.

Optional F.S. Road 462 is short and fun.

Trail crosses New River twice.

F.S. Road 41 winds through foothills.

Shady spot north of Waypoint 03.

Washed out section of road.

New River Canyon 14

Getting There: From Phoenix, head north on Interstate 17 to Table Mesa Road, Exit 236. Bear right and head east on wide dirt road.

Staging/Camping: After you exit, you'll see a large parking area on the south side of Table Mesa Road. Park near sign for state trust land to avoid private property. Camping is allowed on state land, but not many people camp here. If you do, make sure you pack out your trash. A STATE TRUST LAND PERMIT is required on this trail.

Difficulty: Moderate. Steep rocky climbs and washed-out conditions. Two water crossings. River is often dry but can be deep after heavy rains. Trail is in remote backcountry; don't go alone.

Highlights: An in-and-out trail which accesses scenic high desert. Because it's close to Phoenix, it makes a great day trip. Trip can be shortened by skipping Forest Roads 37 and 17, or extended by continuing east to F.S. 24. (F.S. 24 is a larger forest road with more traffic and requires "MC" license plate.)

Trail Description: Don't be mislead by signs along first part of trail that say "ABSOLUTELY NO ATVs." If you stay on Table Mesa Road and have a state trust land permit, it is legal to proceed to forest boundary. Bear left through gate at 1-mile point; do not go right into a private ranch.

Once you reach forest boundary, road becomes F.S. 41. At this point, maintenance ends and the road gets rougher. Trail damage is worse in a few places where a fire occurred in 2005. At one point, the road is completely washed away; however, a manageable bypass has formed. Trip north on F.S. 37 is steeper with deep ruts and washed-out sections (frankly, this is what makes the trail fun). Trip south on F.S. 17 is mildly rocky and climbs toward a high plateau. It finally deteriorates to a point where it is unsafe to proceed. A shady spot just north of Waypoint 03 is a great place for lunch.

Time & Distance: Trip as described totals 43 miles. Allow 4 to 5 hours. Explore other roads to extend day.

Services: None on trail. Closest services are in town of New River, south at Exit 232.

Directions: *(Shadowed portion of trail is described here.)*

WP	Mile	Action
01	0.0	N33° 58.12´ W112° 07.52´ Head east on Table Mesa Road from staging area.
	1.0	Turn left through marked gate bypassing a private ranch. (Right is road to private ranch.)
	2.7	Stay left of gravel pit.
	4.1	Cattle guard marks forest boundary. Road becomes F.S. 41.
02	4.2	N33° 58.33´ W112° 03.79´ Bear right on more traveled road.
	5.1	Follow rocky road uphill past clearing.
	7.3	Cross river.
	7.4	Cross river again. Driver's choice after you cross river. (Right is easier.)
	9.2	First of several short rocky sections.
	11.5	Continue straight at water tank and dilapidated cabin.
	12.1	At washed-out section of trail, bear left down steep bank and follow newly formed road as it circles right back to original road.
03	13.4	N34° 00.57´ W111° 57.28´ Turn left on to F.S. Road 37. Road twists and turns heading north.
	13.5	Shady spot near river on right.
04	16.7	N34° 02.62´ W111° 57.02´ Turn around and return to Waypoint 03. (Optional and more challenging F.S. 462 goes right.)
03	20.0 Reset	Bear left and continue on F.S. Road 41 heading east as road climbs through foothills.
	2.4	Continue straight where F.S. 374 joins from left.
	2.7	Continue straight where F.S. 374 joins from right. (Optional shortcut to F.S. 17.)
05	2.8	N34° 00.42´ W111° 54.96´ At bottom of hill, make hard right on F.S. 17.
	4.0	Continue straight on more traveled F.S. 17. (Right is F.S. 3201 which eventually dead ends.)
06	4.8	N33° 59.39´ W111° 56.21´ End of trail; return to start. (Road continues up mountain but deteriorates badly. Author turned around here.)

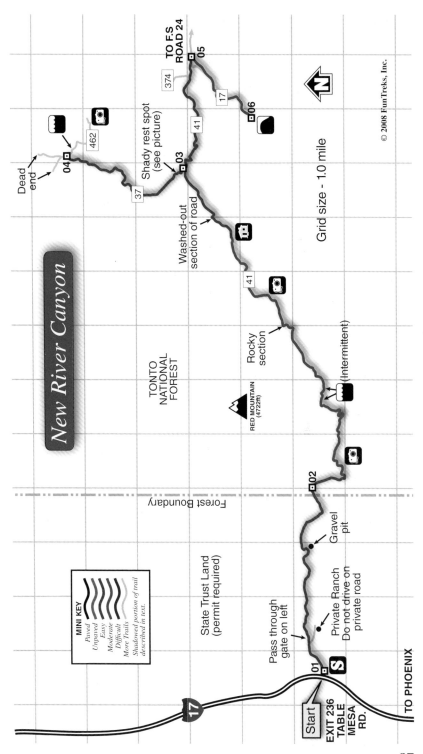

New River Canyon

MINI KEY
Paved
Unpaved
Easy
Moderate
Difficult
More Trails
Shadowed portion of trail described in text.

TONTO NATIONAL FOREST

RED MOUNTAIN (4722ft)

Rocky section

Washed-out section of road

Shady rest spot (see picture)

Dead end

TO F.S ROAD 24

Grid size - 1.0 mile

© 2008 FunTreks, Inc.

N

Forest Boundary

State Trust Land (permit required)

Pass through gate on left

Gravel pit

Private Ranch Do not drive on private road

(Intermittent)

Start
EXIT 236 TABLE MESA RD.

TO PHOENIX

87

Just inside main entrance next to Highway 60 at mile marker 207.

Information board on Rt. 11 at 0.4 miles.

Typical trail where it crosses sandy wash.

Pass through this gate at Waypoint 03 and head west.

Typical terrain is flat and passes through scattered saguaro cacti.

Desert Wells Multiuse Area

Getting There: From Phoenix, take Highway 60 east towards Apache Junction. After Apache Junction, continue southeast on Highway 60 about 7 more miles. Entrance to Desert Wells Multiuse Area is on right at mile marker 207. This area once had over a dozen entry points, but new construction in the area now limits entry to only three points. Besides the main gate, you can enter south of mile marker 150 on Highway 79 and, at one point, on the west side (see map).

Staging/Camping: When you turn into Desert Wells Multiuse Area, you'll be on Route 11. This route is very wide and straight. You can park and unload anywhere along this road. We unloaded immediately near Highway 60 and started our mileage at that point. To camp, drive in about 0.5 miles past the information board.

Difficulty: The route described here is the easiest trail in this book. Trails are fairly flat with occasional dips across small washes. The area is huge and route-finding can be confusing. We covered only a small portion of the area, but still rode over 29 miles. If there are moderate or difficult challenges, we didn't find them.

Highlights: A great place to bring the family to learn how to ride. Area is very easy to find and is close to the east side of Phoenix and Apache Junction. Very open with lots of room to camp. Easy to keep track of your kids if they stay near your campsite. However, if they venture too far away, they could easily get lost in this vast area. Area is somewhat utilitarian and not very scenic.

Time & Distance: Loop route described here measures 29.1 miles. Allow 2 to 4 hours depending upon riding speed.

Trail Description: Route consists of two large loops connected in a figure-8 pattern and one side trip with another small loop. The trail covers the northern one third of the Desert Wells Multiuse Area. There is no particular significance to this route, other than we tried to follow trails that looked interesting.

Services: Full services in Apache Junction and Florence. Closest gas is in a shopping center on Highway 60 near mile marker 202. Area is fast-growing, so expect more nearby services in the future.

Directions: *(Shadowed portion of trail is described here.)*

WP	Mile	Action
01	0.0	*N33° 18.42′ W111° 24.46′* From near Hwy. 60, head southwest on Rt. 11. Go past kiosk after 0.4 miles.
02	2.1	*N33° 17.55′ W111° 26.23′* Continue straight. (Rt. 13 joins on left.
	2.3	Continue straight under power lines as route changes to Rt. 1, which swings south along fenceline.
03	3.9	*N33° 16.14′ W111° 26.49′* Turn right through gate and follow Rt. 2 west.
04	6.6	*N33° 15.52′ W112° 29.07′* Bear right at Y on Rt. 26 (not marked) and go past corral (on your right).
	7.4	Turn right along fence line. Road heads north then begins to curve right away from fence.
05	8.0	*N33° 16.34′ W111° 29.60′* Turn left across ruts and head west back towards fence again, then continue north along fence.
	8.2	Turn right away from fence and head east.
	9.6	Make a hard right turn. (Straight is closed to motorized vehicles.)
05	10.9	Stay left along fence, then east over same route.
04	12.3	Return to Wpt. 04 after corral and turn right on Rt. 26 (not marked).
	15.2	Bear left at T and head north.
03	15.9	Turn right through gate and continue east on Rt. 2.
	17.2	Continue straight where 24 goes right and 15 goes left. Rt. 2 soon changes to Rt. 22.
06	20.1	*N33° 16.64′ W111° 22.31′* Turn left on gravel road.
	20.4	Turn left on Rt. 2 away from Highway 60.
	22.1	Bear right on Rt. 12 along power lines.
07	22.5	*N33° 16.61′ W111° 24.27′* Turn right on Rt. 13.
	24.8	Stay right. Rt. 13 splits two ways.
08	25.7	*N33° 16.71′ W111° 25.21′* Turn right on Rt. 13 where Rt. 15 goes left.
02	27.0	Return to Wpt. 02 and turn right on Rt. 11.
01	29.1	Return to start near Highway 60.

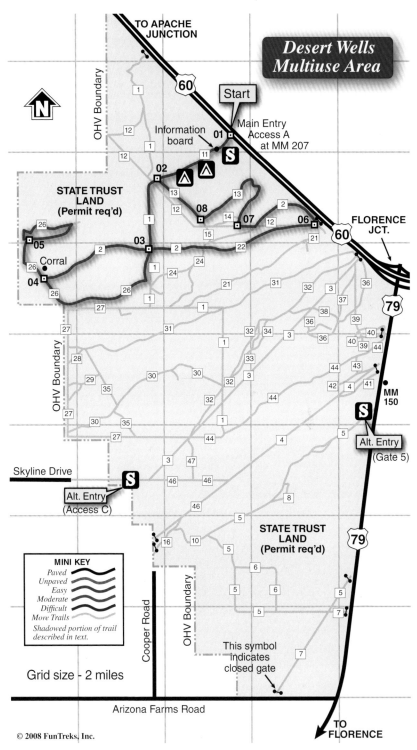

Desert Wells
Multiuse Area

TO APACHE
JUNCTION

60

N

OHV Boundary

Start

Main Entry
Access A
at MM 207

Information
board

01

S

11

STATE TRUST
LAND
(Permit req'd)

02

13

13

08

12

07

14

06

21

02

FLORENCE
JCT.

60

79

26

05

03

02

24

15

22

12

Corral

26

26

04

26

24

21

31

32

3

36

27

26

1

24

37

27

31

1

32

34

3

36

38

36

39

40

44

OHV Boundary

28

29

35

30

30

33

52

3

44

43

40

39

44

41

42

4

MM
150

27

30

35

32

44

S

27

1

Alt. Entry
(Gate 5)

4

5

Skyline Drive

3

47

S

46

46

Alt. Entry
(Access C)

46

8

5

MINI KEY

Paved
Unpaved
Easy
Moderate
Difficult
More Trails

16

10

5

STATE TRUST
LAND
(Permit req'd)

79

Shadowed portion of trail
described in text.

6

5

6

5

Grid size - 2 miles

Cooper Road

OHV Boundary

5

7

This symbol
indicates
closed gate

7

Arizona Farms Road

TO
FLORENCE

© 2008 FunTreks, Inc.

Staging area at entrance to Agua Fria National Monument. (Check for maps at kiosk.)

Hidden petroglyphs.

Side trip at Waypoint 04 leads to this stone cabin.

One of many stone walls at Pueblo la Plata.

Watch for Gila Monsters crossing road.

High point of trip.

View from west side of Sheep Bridge.

Bloody Basin, Sheep Bridge 16

Getting There: From Phoenix, head north on Interstate 17 to Exit 259 and bear right on Bloody Basin Road into Agua Fria National Monument. Staging area is just around the corner after pavement ends.

Staging/Camping: Plenty of room to park in staging area, but no toilet. One is located 6.2 miles east. Better camping is available along Bloody Basin Road as you drive east. Watch for wide spots along the road. Before leaving staging area, check information board for regulations to Agua Fria National Monument. Sign-in box usually has maps inside. Please pack out all trash.

Difficulty: First 11 miles is inside Agua Fria National Monument, where road is well maintained. However, road can become muddy when wet and even impassable in spots during long wet spells. As you continue east into Tonto National Forest, the road gets progressively narrower and rockier, but is still rated easy. Side trips to archaeological sites are rutted in places and impassable when wet.

Highlights: Sheep Bridge at end of trail is an impressive sight. Bridge spans wide Verde River with a 476-ft. walkway. Original bridge, built in 1943, was rebuilt in 1989 to look like the old bridge. Today the bridge is used for pedestrian traffic only. A hidden concrete-enclosed hot spring is purportedly located in thick brush just north of the west side of the bridge. (Author's note: We didn't know the location of the hot spring at the time of our visit, and couldn't find it. Later, online, we found the location. We hope to return someday to get pictures.) Side trips at Wpts. 02 and 03 lead to interesting archaeological sites. Side trip at Waypoint 03 also has a long cliff area with petroglyphs.

Time & Distance: This is a very long trip measuring 38 miles one way. If you ride all three side trips at Waypoints 02, 03 and 04, you add about 14 miles. Although you move along swiftly, you should allow a full day for this adventure.

Trail Description: You'll head southeast across rolling, open land and enter Tonto National Forest. A good road climbs gradually to a high point with broad views, then begins a long descent towards the Verde River. Verde River is usually too deep to cross.

Services: Modern vault toilet at 6.2 miles. No other services.

Directions: *(Shadowed portion of trail is described here.)*

WP	Mile	Action
01	0.0	N34° 17.00´ W112° 07.12´ Head south from staging area on wide Bloody Basin Road 9269.
	1.6	Continue straight where 9005 goes right. Good camp spot here.
	5.3	Continue straight. (Gate on left goes to private ranch.) Cross stream at bottom of hill.
	6.2	Vault toilet with small parking area on right.
02	8.5	N34° 14.13´ W112° 01.76´ Continue straight. (Optional: Road 9023 goes left 1.3 miles to Pueblo la Plata, large ruin of prehistoric Indian village. Impassable when wet.)
03	11.1	N34° 13.67´ W111° 59.50´ Continue straight past kiosk. (Optional: Follow 9014 right five miles to Indian petroglyphs and more pueblo ruins. Impassable when wet. See map.)
	11.5	Cross boundary into Tonto National Forest.
	18.3	High point with great views begins descent towards Verde River.
04	21.9	N34° 11.11´ W111° 51.49´ Continue straight. (Optional: Right 0.6 miles on F.S. 578 and 3170 goes to interesting stone cabin.)
	25.3	Shady camp spot on right by stream.
05	26.1	N34° 09.34´ W111° 49.32´ Continue straight. (Cave Creek Road, F.S. 24 goes south. ATVs should have "MC" plate to travel on this road.)
	27.0	Continue straight. F.S. Road 16 goes left. More creek crossings follow as road gets rougher.
06	38.0	N34° 04.68´ W111° 42.49´ Road winds downhill, eventually reaching Sheep Bridge. This bridge is for foot traffic only. Road continues south past bridge and crosses river; however, water is seldom shallow enough to cross on ATV. Just before the bridge, a rocky road goes left downhill to sandbar next to river. Camp in existing spots with stone fire rings. Bugs can be intense in the summer. Take insect repellent.

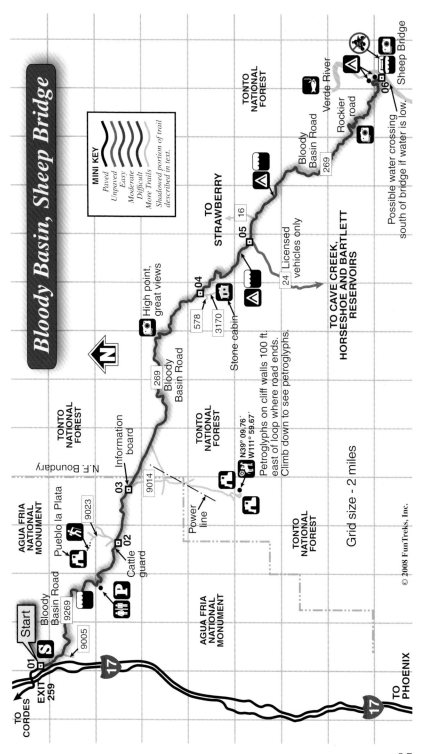

Bloody Basin, Sheep Bridge

MINI KEY
Paved
Unpaved
Easy
Moderate
Difficult
More Trails
Shadowed portion of trail
described in text.

TO CORDES

EXIT 259

TO PHOENIX

Start

01

Bloody Basin Road

9269

9005

02 Cattle guard

P

03 Information board

N.F. Boundary

AGUA FRIA NATIONAL MONUMENT

Pueblo la Plata

9023

TONTO NATIONAL FOREST

9014

Power line

Petroglyphs on cliff walls 100 ft.
east of loop where road ends.
Climb down to see petroglyphs.

N39° 09.76'
W111° 59.67'

TONTO NATIONAL FOREST

TONTO NATIONAL FOREST

AGUA FRIA NATIONAL MONUMENT

269 Bloody Basin Road

04

578

3170

Stone cabin

High point, great views

TO STRAWBERRY

05 16

24 Licensed vehicles only

TO CAVE CREEK, HORSESHOE AND BARTLETT RESERVOIRS

Grid size - 2 miles

TONTO NATIONAL FOREST

269 Bloody Basin Road

Rockier road

Verde River

06 Sheep Bridge

Possible water crossing
south of bridge if water is low.

© 2008 FunTreks, Inc.

95

Good camp spot at 2.5 miles. Transport vehicles can drive to this point.

View from ore chute above mill.

Tumbling chamber in which ore was pulverized.

Road enters creek at 4.9 miles.

Trail becomes very difficult after mine.

Parts of trail follow creek.

Sunflower Mine ⟨17⟩

Getting There: From east side of Phoenix, take Highway 87 north and turn left on road marked to Sycamore Creek/Mt. Ord, 0.6 miles past mile marker 222. Follow paved road downhill 1.1 miles and turn right on F.S. 201.

Staging/Camping: After you turn right on 201, you'll see a wide area on the left for staging. To camp, continue another 2.5 miles, following trail directions. You'll see camp spots on left before creek crossing. Like all national forests, you may camp anywhere along the trail up to 14 days. Try to find a place where others have already camped.

Difficulty: First half of route to mine is moderately steep and rocky. Second half of route requires maneuvering over large boulders, then climbing an extremely steep, rocky hill. This portion is for advanced riders only. Don't attempt this hill alone. We found it prudent to use a safety line on front of ATV to avoid flipping over backwards. *UTVs can make it to the mine with some effort, but should stop there.*

Highlights: Visit historic Sunflower Mine (a.k.a. National Mine). When you reach the mill, you'll see a giant steel pipe that tumbled a reddish-brown ore called cinnabar. The resulting fine particles were burned in vertical furnaces with coke to produce mercury gas. The gas liquified after being cooled in giant U-shape tubes. Most of this equipment is still standing inside a large dilapidated wooden building. Large mines are scattered on hillsides around the mill. Never enter a mine regardless of how safe it may appear.

Time & Distance: Round trip to mine and back is 11.8 miles and takes 3 to 4 hours. If you ride the entire loop, it measures 13.6 miles and takes 4 to 5 hours.

Trail Description: The fun begins when you begin climbing up F.S. 25A. This road is heavily rutted and steep, but fun to ride. Where the trail follows the creek before the mine, it is a bit rocky, but nothing like after the mine. Please don't continue on the loop portion of route after the mine unless you can handle an extreme challenge. Make sure you travel with a buddy who can spot for you as needed.

Services: Nothing nearby. Head back to outskirts of Phoenix or north to Payson for full services.

Directions: *(Shadowed portion of trail is described here.)*

WP	Mile	Action
01	**0.0**	*N33° 55.89´ W111° 27.82´* From staging area near Sycamore Creek Road, head north on well graded F.S. 201.
02	**1.2**	*N33° 56.62´ W111° 27.02´* Cross cattle guard and bear left downhill on F.S. 25.
	2.5	Continue straight across creek. Good camp spots on left.
03	**3.9**	*N33° 56.49´ W111° 28.97´* Bear right uphill on F.S. 25A. Rougher road climbs steeply, then levels off across high shelf.
	4.9	Descend to bottom of hill and follow along rocky creek to right.
	5.1	Cross short steel bridge.
	5.3	Continue straight. (Left dead ends.)
04	**5.6**	*N33° 57.46´ W111° 29.50´* Make a sharp left turn uphill to reach Sunflower Mill.
	5.8	Stay left. You'll see the mill below. (Right uphill, at this point, leads to mines.)
05	**5.9**	*N33° 57.29´ W111° 29.67´* Road ends at bottom of hill. Walk short distance back to mine. Return to Wpt. 04.
04	**6.2** *Reset*	Turn left to continue. Trail becomes extremely difficult and is for advanced riders only. Novice riders go back.
	0.8	Trail follows creek over very large rocks.
06	**0.9**	*N33° 57.94´ W111° 28.88´* Turn hard right uphill out of creek on F.S. 3722. Begin extremely steep, rocky climb. Consider using safety strap to avoid flipping backwards.
	1.4	Stay right.
07	**1.7**	*N33° 58.08´ W111° 28.26´* Roads converge at camp spot. Bear slightly right downhill on F.S. 201A.
	1.9	Driver's choice down steep, rocky descent. Right easier.
	3.1	After narrow ledge road, drop downhill and cross creek. On other side of creek, turn hard right. Trail soon turns left up one final long steep hill.
08	**3.8**	*N33° 58.06´ W111° 27.00´* Intersect with F.S. 201 and bear right on easy road.
02	**6.2**	Loop completed. Continue straight across cattle guard and head south on 201 back to staging area.
01	**7.4**	Return to starting point.

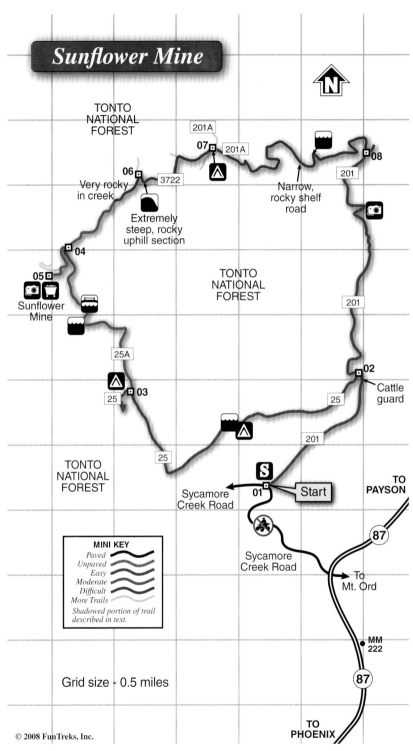

Sunflower Mine

TONTO NATIONAL FOREST

201A
07 201A

06 3722

Very rocky in creek

Extremely steep, rocky uphill section

04

05

Sunflower Mine

25A

25 **03**

TONTO NATIONAL FOREST

Narrow, rocky shelf road

08

201

201

02

Cattle guard

25

201

25

TONTO NATIONAL FOREST

S
01 Start

Sycamore Creek Road

TO PAYSON

Sycamore Creek Road

To Mt. Ord

87

MM 222

87

MINI KEY
Paved
Unpaved
Easy
Moderate
Difficult
More Trails
Shadowed portion of trail
described in text.

Grid size - 0.5 miles

TO PHOENIX

© 2008 FunTreks, Inc.

Creek crossing after Waypoint 02.

Fun ride through sandy wash.

Difficult boulder field at 1.6 miles may be too difficult for some riders.

Steep descent from Log Corral.

F.S. Road 393 was in need of repair.

Log Corral to Bartlett Lake

Getting There: From east side of Phoenix, take Highway 87 north and turn left 0.7 miles past mile marker 212. Continue downhill on wide F.S. 3456 to staging and camping just around the corner.

Staging/Camping: An irregular shaped sandy area in the trees next to the creek. F.S. 1333 goes right here through the camping area and heads northwest. Dispersed camping only, no services. Pack out trash.

Difficulty: A half-mile section that begins at 1.6 miles follows a narrow creek. This section starts with a difficult boulder field then becomes jungle-like, with tight brush and fallen trees nearly blocking the route. We found the westerly descent from Waypoint 03 very steep, washed out, and tippy in places. F.S. 393 appeared to be a major road, but on 5/30/08, it was washed away in places and barely wide enough for an ATV to squeeze by. Since this road is needed to maintain a power line, it will likely be repaired someday soon. Verde River, at end of route, is usually too deep to cross. *Significant rock obstacles and narrow places make this trail unsuitable for UTVs.*

Highlights: Incredible fun if you like challenge, variety and surprises. The sandy wash that climbs the east side is an absolute blast. If F.S. 393 is not repaired, there may be sections of the road that completely wash out. Great scenery on the west side of Log Corral as you descend toward the lake and traverse along its southern edge.

Time & Distance: Almost 25 miles if you make it all the way to the river and back. Allow 4 to 5 hours depending on conditions.

Trail Description: Trail starts by winding back and forth across a rocky creek, then turns northwest up a lesser side canyon. After a half mile of slow-going obstacles, you begin a 3-mile section of easy, fun, twisting wash. You cross a high ridge at Log Corral and begin a steep descent to the lake. If you go straight at Waypoint 04, it ends at the lake. You can end your trip here, or check out conditions of F.S. 393 across the south end of lake. If you are lucky, you might make it all the way to the Verde River, as we did. During an extreme dry spell, you might even be able to cross the river to a Forest Service campground on other side.

Services: Nothing nearby. Head back to outskirts of Phoenix.

Directions: *(Shadowed portion of trail is described here.)*

WP	Mile	Action
01	0.0	*N33° 47.80´ W111° 29.65´* Head southwest from staging area on rough road that runs along north side of wash. You can ride in the wash, too, but it may be blocked in places.
	0.6	Canyon on right is not the one you want. Continue straight.
02	0.9	*N33° 47.40´ W111° 30.30´* Bear right through wooded area, cross creek and head northwest up side canyon.
	1.0	Pass through gate and close it.
	1.6	Very difficult boulder field. (We saw UTVs turning around at this obstacle.) Several very narrow spots follow.
	2.1	Worst is over. Begin gradual climb up wide, sandy wash. Wash meanders back and forth and is great fun.
03	5.0	*N33° 48.41´ W111° 33.67´* Reach top of ridge at log corral. First views of lake. Trail is steep and rutted as you descend other side.
04	8.3	*N33° 49.40´ W111° 36.33´* Bear left uphill on F.S. 393. Straight ends at lake. (Note: On 5/30/08, trail was badly washed out. Sections of the trail were barely wide enough for an ATV to squeeze through. This road will likely be repaired in the future.)
05	12.1	*N33° 48.35´ W111° 38.96´* Main trail goes left. A lesser road had formed to the right that went down to the river. If road is repaired, stay left. You can turn around anytime, since the river is likely too deep to get across.
01	24.6	Return to start.

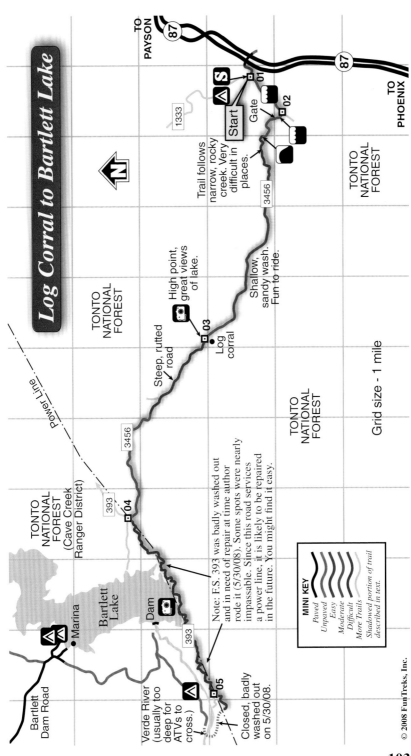

Log Corral to Bartlett Lake

TO PAYSON

87

TO PHOENIX

87

S △

Start

Gate

01

02

Trail follows narrow, rocky creek. Very difficult in places.

1333

3456

N

TONTO NATIONAL FOREST

TONTO NATIONAL FOREST

High point, great views of lake.

03

Log corral

Steep, rutted road

Shallow, sandy wash. Fun to ride.

3456

TONTO NATIONAL FOREST

Grid size - 1 mile

Power Line

TONTO NATIONAL FOREST (Cave Creek Ranger District)

393

04

Marina

Bartlett Lake

Dam

Bartlett Dam Road

Verde River (usually too deep for ATVs to cross.)

393

05

Closed, badly washed out on 5/30/08.

Note: F.S. 393 was badly washed out and in need of repair at time author rode it (5/30/08). Some spots were nearly impassable. Since this road services a power line, it is likely to be repaired in the future. You might find it easy.

MINI KEY
Paved
Unpaved
Easy
Moderate
Difficult
More Trails
Shadowed portion of trail described in text.

© 2008 FunTreks, Inc.

103

Popular trail for guided tours. Shown here, guide (on ATV) leads group of desert cars.

Waypoint 03, start of F.S. 1851.

Stay off abused areas like this.

Heading west into foothills from Wpt. 06.

View from near end of trail. Four Peaks top left. Sugarloaf Mountain at right.

Sycamore Ck, Sugarloaf Mtn

Getting There: From east side of Phoenix, head north on Highway 87. Watch for F.S. 403 on the west side of highway between mile markers 200 and 201. You need to turn left, but new construction may have eliminated a cut-through at this point. If you can't turn left, continue another 3 miles and circle back at Four Peaks Road.

You can also access this trail from Four Peaks Road. Bear left and head west on F.S. 402. A tight "S" curve at 2.7 miles marks the connecting point with F.S. 1851 (not marked). From here, head north on 402 or south on 1851.

Staging/Camping: Plenty of room to park and unload at F.S. 403. Drive in a short distance away from the highway to find a camp spot. The alternate starting point at 402 has no defined staging area; however, you'll find plenty of wide places to park as you drive in.

Difficulty: Main route has a few steep, rocky places but most of this trail is easy. Plenty of side obstacles if you are looking for more challenge. Route-finding is confusing at times.

Highlights: This route serves as an introduction to a vast area of trails open to motorized recreation. Ride this route first, then choose an area you like best. We tried to select routes that had relatively few whoops.

We rode a portion of Ironwood Wash west of Waypoint 02 (off map) in an attempt to make a loop connecting with Waypoint 07; however, the giant, unrelenting whoops were absolutely insane. We found them no fun at all and turned back after 2 miles.

Time & Distance: Out and back measures 19 miles as described here. Allow 3 to 4 hours without side trips. You could easily spend several days exploring everything available.

Trail Description: Head north on 403 over mild whoops to Sycamore Creek, a wide, flat, sandy creek bed (usually dry). Follow creek bed northeast short distance, then cut through to F.S. 402 via unmarked F.S 1851. Stay north on 402 to sheep camp, after which, a rough trail follows creek north. Leave creek heading west from Waypoint 06 and climb fun road into foothills. Views at top.

Services: Nothing nearby. Head back to the outskirts of Phoenix. Four Peaks staging area, on the east side of Highway 87, has a vault toilet.

Directions: *(Shadowed portion of trail is described here.)*

WP	Mile	Action
01	**0.0**	*N33° 38.49´ W111° 32.57´* From staging area, head west on F.S. 403. Trail curves north and follows a sandy wash with moderate whoops.
02	**2.5**	*N33° 39.93´ W111° 33.82´* Turn right into Sycamore Creek, a gigantic, flat wash (typically dry).
03	**3.0**	*N33° 40.18´ W111° 33.49´* Turn right uphill out of Sycamore Creek. Follow dished-out wash as it gradually climbs. (Lots of fun side trails in this area.)
	3.5	Continue straight in main wash past cattle guard.
	3.7	Stay left and climb steeply over a low ridge.
	4.3	Continue northeast. Make no turns as two large washes cross on diagonal.
	4.7	Stay in main wash heading almost due north towards distinctive Sugarloaf Mountain.
04	**5.1**	*N33° 41.16´ W111° 32.20´* Intersect with major F.S. Road 402. Road parallels wash, in which you have been traveling, and continues north. **Please make note of this point because it is very easy to miss on return trip.** (If you turn right on 402, it heads east to Highway 87, an alternate entry point.)
05	**5.8**	*N33° 41.70´ W111° 32.35´* Road swings left across creek at concrete wall to sheep camp on other side. Bear right at sheep camp and continue north following main creek. You'll cross back and forth several times. Be aware that flash floods are always possible.
06	**7.7**	*N33° 43.08´ W111° 32.62´* Bear left out of main wash on F.S. 1856 and head west.
	8.4	Wash splits, stay left. Trail gets narrower and begins to climb.
	9.1	Trail swings right at tight switchback. Great views looking east.
07	**9.5**	*N33° 43.38´ W111° 34.06´* Gate before T intersection. Turn around and return the way you came. (Option: You can continue through gate, where a left turn eventually heads south via Ironwood Wash back to Sycamore Creek near Waypoint 02. This is a long trip with an endless number of monotonous, annoying whoops.)

106

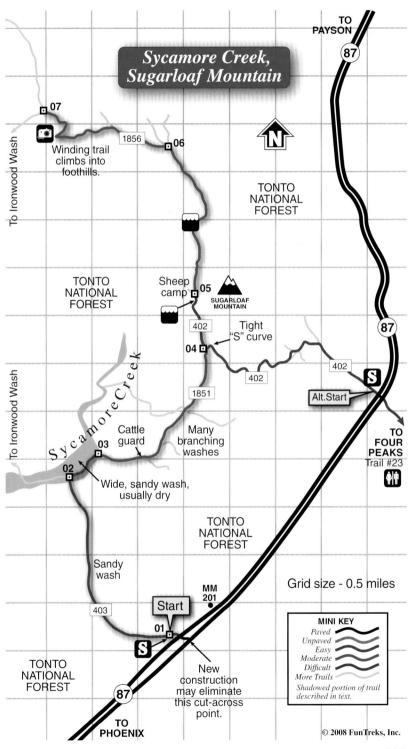

Sycamore Creek, Sugarloaf Mountain

TO PAYSON
87

07

1856

06

Winding trail climbs into foothills.

TONTO NATIONAL FOREST

N

TONTO NATIONAL FOREST

Sheep camp

05

SUGARLOAF MOUNTAIN

402

Tight "S" curve

04

402

402

87

S

Alt. Start

1851

Cattle guard

Many branching washes

TO FOUR PEAKS
Trail #23

03

Sycamore Creek

To Ironwood Wash

02

Wide, sandy wash, usually dry

TONTO NATIONAL FOREST

Sandy wash

Grid size - 0.5 miles

403

Start

MM 201

01

S

New construction may eliminate this cut-across point.

TONTO NATIONAL FOREST

87

TO PHOENIX

MINI KEY
Paved
Unpaved
Easy
Moderate
Difficult
More Trails
Shadowed portion of trail described in text.

© 2008 FunTreks, Inc.

107

Trail starts here west of main parking area.

South half of F.S. 1863 follows sandy wash.

Favorite area for guided tours.

Lots of twists and turns.

F.S. 13 is hilly in places.

Rolls OHV Area, North

Getting There: From east side of Phoenix, head north on Beeline Highway 87. Turn right on Four Peaks Road just before mile marker 204. Drive east on F.S. 143 about 0.7 miles to large parking lot with vault toilet on right.

Staging/Camping: On weekends, main parking lot fills up quickly. It is very congested and people squeeze in anywhere they can fit. Better parking and camping is available if you continue several miles east on F.S. 143. In addition, F.S. 401 has some great camp spots at various points along the road as you head south.

Difficulty: A mix of soft sand and hard-packed undulating surfaces. F.S. 13, which runs east and west, is narrow, very twisty, with lots of short climbs and descents. F.S. 143 is a wide gravel road with fast moving traffic, so use caution.

Highlights: Trails are easier at the northern end of Rolls OHV Area and are better suited for kids and novice riders. Route-finding is relatively simple compared to the complex network of trails farther south. You can also start at the Pobrecito Staging Area off Bush Highway and head north on F.S. 13. To ride all day on easy trails, head east into the mountains on F.S. 143 (see Trail #23 in this book).

Time & Distance: The course described here measures about 15 miles and takes 1 to 2 hours depending on riding skills. You can shorten the course to 9 miles by skipping F.S. 1832 and returning directly to start from Waypoint 6.

Trail Description: Trail heads southwest and drops into a wide, sandy wash, then turns east on F.S. 13, one of the most popular routes in the Rolls OHV Area. This trail is just the right width for ATVs and has lots of hills and tight curves. You'll often see guided ATV tours on this trail. You'll leave F.S.13 at Waypoint 04 and head north on easier 1343. It connects to F.S. 401, which connects to F.S. 143. You can return to staging area on 143, or extend the trip by turning south on 1832 and looping back on 1863, in the opposite direction you rode it earlier.

Services: Vault toilet at staging area. Head back towards Phoenix on Highway 87 and Bush Highway for all other services.

Directions: *(Shadowed portion of trail is described here.)*

WP	Mile	Action
01	0.0	*N33° 40.17′ W111° 29.75′* From main parking lot at toilet, head southwest on wide, undulating road.
	0.5	Bear slightly left uphill on lesser road.
	2.0	Trail follows sandy wash due south.
	2.6	Driver's choice. Wash splits, but soon comes back together.
02	2.9	*N33° 38.43′ W111° 31.56′* Bear left on narrower F.S. 13. (Right goes south along ridge 3.8 miles to Pobrecito Staging Area.)
	3.5	Continue east on 13. (Don't turn right.)
03	3.8	*N33° 38.36′ W111° 30.66′* Follow wide spot around to left, then turn right, continuing east on 13.
	4.5	Continue east on 13. (1863 goes south.)
04	5.5	*N33° 38.24′ W111° 29.22′* Continue straight, heading north, on 1343. (You leave 13 at this point.)
	6.9	Continue straight.
05	7.6	*N33° 39.91′ W111° 28.40′* Turn left on larger F.S. 401.
	7.7	Bear left on main road 143.
06	8.4 *Reset*	*N33° 40.14′ W111° 29.08′* Bear left on 1832. (To go directly back to start, continue straight 0.7 miles on 143.)
	1.4	Stay left.
03	2.7	Bear right. You are now back on 13.
	3.0	Continue west.
02	3.6	Turn right and head north on 1863 and retrace your earlier route back to start.
01	6.5	Return to staging area.

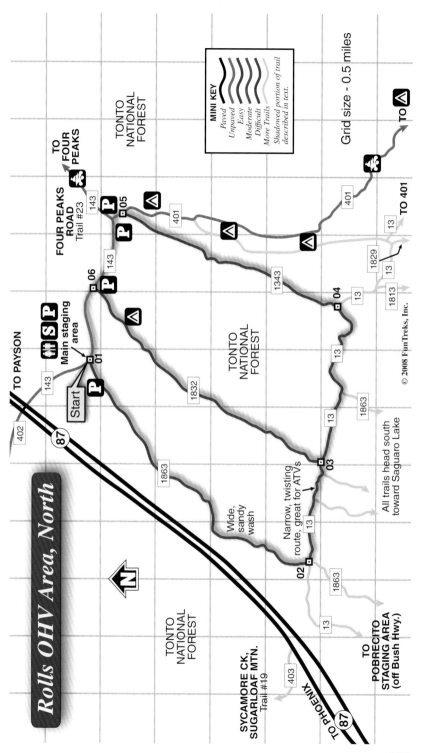

Rolls OHV Area, North

N

TO PAYSON

TO FOUR PEAKS

FOUR PEAKS ROAD
Trail #23

TONTO NATIONAL FOREST

TONTO NATIONAL FOREST

TONTO NATIONAL FOREST

MINI KEY
Paved
Unpaved
Easy
Moderate
Difficult
More Trails
Shadowed portion of trail described in text.

Grid size - 0.5 miles

Main staging area

Start

Wide, sandy wash

Narrow, twisting route, great for ATVs

All trails head south toward Saguaro Lake

SYCAMORE CK, SUGARLOAF MTN.
Trail #19

TO POBRECITO STAGING AREA
(off Bush Hwy.)

TO PHOENIX

© 2008 FunTreks, Inc.

87

402

143

143

143

143

01

06

05

04

03

02

401

401

1343

1832

1863

1863

1863

1863

1829

1813

13

13

13

13

13

13

13

13

TO 401

TO

111

Staging at Pobrecito Recreation Site.

High point of trail at Waypoint 05.

Steep climb just before first cove.

Stopping for lunch at first cove.

Small beach at Waypoint 08.

Rolls OHV Area, South

Getting There: Take Bush Highway east from Phoenix past Saguaro Lake. Just north of Butcher Jones Road, turn right near mile marker 34. Continue east past boat parking area. Follow dirt road short distance to staging area behind parking lot.

Staging/Camping: Staging area doubles as camping area. NOTE: At time of this writing, no special permit (other than normal registration) is needed to ride and camp in Rolls OHV Area; however, Tonto National Forest is considering a permit similar to what is required at Bulldog Canyon, Trail #24. Best to call ahead to check status.

Difficulty: Most of route is easy to moderate. The difficulty begins as you near the lake and cross from cove to cove. Washes are separated by high ridges which are very steep. To find a suitable crossing point, you may have to head away from the lake, where ridges are lower.

Highlights: You'll start at the west-side staging area and circle all the way around to the east side, then climb to a high point with great views of the entire area. From here you'll descend to the easternmost coves, where you'll find relative solitude and spectacular views. This fun-packed route is one of the most enjoyable in the OHV area.

Time & Distance: Round trip out and back is over 26 miles. Allow 3 to 5 hours, plus extra time to explore numerous other enticing roads that branch off.

Trail Description: Head north on F.S. 13 along a rocky ridge, then follow 13 east through center of OHV area. This stretch is narrower with lots of twists, short climbs and descents. At Waypoint 04, you turn south and follow a high ridge, then descend steeply toward the lake. Explore a variety of coves, then loop back to Waypoint 05. From here, return to staging area over same route as you entered.

It is possible to return a different way, but it requires heading east and winding back and forth on a network of confusing roads that cross many more ridges. Eventually, you'll still have to head north to connect to F.S. 13. It doesn't save time, but it's quite an adventure.

Services: Vault toilet at boat trailer parking area is not part of staging area. Return to outskirts of Phoenix for all services.

Directions: *(Shadowed portion of trail is described here.)*

WP	Mile	Action
01	0.0	N33° 35.70´ W111° 32.53´ From staging area, head north on F.S. 13 along ridge.
	3.8	Trail swings east and drops downhill. Stay left at fork before Waypoint 02.
02	3.9	N33° 38.43´ W111° 31.56´ Continue east on 13 across wide, sandy wash. Ignore roads that go north and south.
03	6.4	N33° 38.24´ W111° 29.22´ Bear right, heading southeast on 13.
	6.8	Stay left downhill on 13 (1813 goes right).
04	7.3	N33° 37.80´ W111° 28.65´ Bear right on 1829. Trail begins gradual climb.
	7.8	Stay left.
05	8.7	N33° 36.95´ W111° 27.86´ Stay left at top of steep, rocky hill. Great views.
	9.7	Steep, rocky descent, then levels out.
06	10.8	N33° 35.28´ W111° 27.54´ Turn hard right and head north before cattle pond.
	11.4	After rocky section, trail enters sandy wash.

WP	Mile	Action
	13.1	Driver's choice. Difficult boulders to left.
	13.2	Canyon ends; go up steep rock face to right.
07	13.3 Reset	N33° 34.43´ W111° 28.92´ High point above coves. Great scenic spot for lunch. Head northeast along ridge.
	0.2	Make sharp left.
	0.3	Make hard right down steep hill and bear right in sandy wash. (Small beach to left.)
	0.5	Turn left uphill out of wash. Stay right at next 2 forks. Left turns go to lake.
	0.8	Stay left towards beach.
08	1.1 Reset	N33° 34.68´ W111° 29.14´ Pass through trees to small sandy beach. Then turn around and follow large wash left.
09	2.1	N33° 36.22´ W111° 28.41´ Watch for cairn on right that marks spot where you climb steep hill out of wash.
05	3.2	Return to high point. Left goes back to start.
01	11.9	Return to staging area.

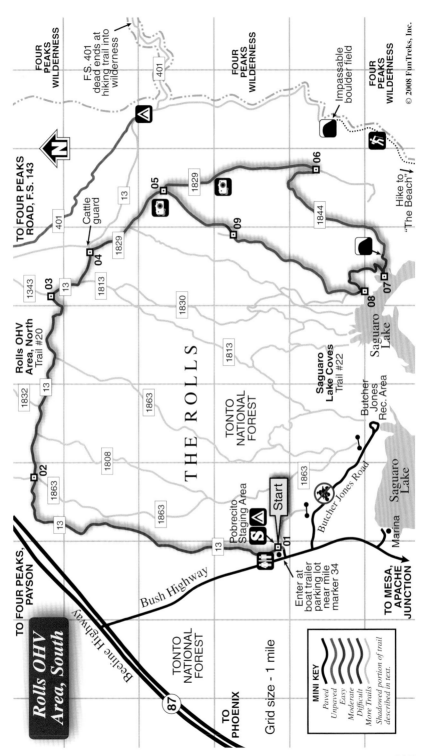

Rolls OHV Area, South

© 2008 FunTreks, Inc.

FOUR PEAKS WILDERNESS

FOUR PEAKS WILDERNESS

FOUR PEAKS WILDERNESS

F.S. 401 dead ends at hiking trail into wilderness

Impassable boulder field

Hike to "The Beach"

TO FOUR PEAKS ROAD, F.S. 143

N

Cattle guard

401

13

1829

04

1829

05

1829

06

09

1844

07

08

03

1343

13

1813

1830

Saguaro Lake

Rolls OHV Area, North Trail #20

1813

THE ROLLS

Saguaro Lake Coves Trail #22

Butcher Jones Rec. Area

1832

13

1863

TONTO NATIONAL FOREST

02

1863

1808

1863

1863

Pobrecito Staging Area

Start

1863

Butcher Jones Road

Saguaro Lake

13

S

01

Marina

TO FOUR PEAKS, PAYSON

Enter at boat trailer parking lot near mile marker 34

TO MESA, APACHE JUNCTION

Bush Highway

Beeline Highway

TONTO NATIONAL FOREST

Grid size - 1 mile

87

TO PHOENIX

MINI KEY
Paved
Unpaved
Easy
Moderate
Difficult
More Trails
Shadowed portion of trail described in text.

Jeepers camping in wide wash at start of trail.

Vehicles park at water's edge at Cove #1.

Great area for UTVs.

In search of not-so-steep hills

"The Beach," boaters and hikers only.

Steep, chewed-up hill at Waypoint 04.

Saguaro Lake Coves

Getting There: Take Bush Highway east from Phoenix to Saguaro Lake. Continue on Bush Highway 0.9 miles past road to marina and turn right on Butcher Jones Road. Go east about 2 miles to loop at end of road and circle around to north end of loop. Here you'll find a gate that leads to a wide, sandy wash. Head north in the wash. (The gate is usually open, but there are rare situations when the Forest Service closes it. A permit system, like at Bulldog Canyon, Trail #24, is being considered for Rolls OHV Area. **IF** this occurs, the Tonto N.F. will likely put a combination lock on this gate.)

Staging/Camping: Butcher Jones Recreation Area is a fee area. You must pass through the gate to reach the non-fee area. Drive in a short distance and park or camp wherever you can find room in the wash.

Difficulty: This part of Rolls OHV Area is really a mixed bag. The washes are easy, but the ridges between the washes are very steep. A few places are chewed up and quite difficult. To avoid the steepest part of each ridge, head north before crossing over. "Competition Hill" (as the Jeepers call it) is on the east side of Cove #1. It is tempting to cross over here to get to Cove #2, immediately on the other side, but it is dangerously steep. Every wash continues north. Some are easy, others have difficult sections. Route-finding is very challenging, but once you get the hang of the terrain, you should be able to find your way around.

Highlights: Visit coves and scenic high points along the north shore of Saguaro Lake. (During our trip, we heard people talking about "The Beach," apparently the granddaddy of all the beaches. After 3 days, we finally found it. Unfortunately, this particular beach is only reachable by hiking or by boat. Route to it is shown on map for Trail #21.)

Time & Distance: As described here, one-way distance to Cove #3 is about 9 miles. You'll spend an hour or two if you don't get sidetracked. You can easily spend a week in the area exploring the vast network of intertwined roads.

Trail Description: This little-known entry point is the shortest way to coves. Zigzag north and south to get over steep ridges between washes. Join boaters on sandy beaches.

Services: Pack a cooler and extra gas. No services nearby.

Directions: *(Shadowed portion of trail is described here.)*

WP	Mile	Action
01	0.0	*N33° 34.65′ W111° 30.85′* From staging area, head north in wide, sandy wash.
	0.6	Stay left in main wash.
02	0.8	*N33° 35.30′ W111° 30.74′* Bear right.
	1.4	Bear right up steep, rough hill.
03	1.5	*N33° 35.73′ W111° 30.34′* At top of hill, bear left along ridge.
	1.8	Turn right. Trail goes east, then south.
04	2.3	*N33° 35.75′ W111° 29.85′* Descend nasty, chewed-up hill and turn right in wash.
05	3.6 Reset	*N33° 34.83′ W111° 29.84′* Reach Cove #1. Enjoy, then turn around and go back up wash.
06	0.8	*N33° 35.42′ W111° 29.86′* Turn right out of wash and cross over another ridge.
07	1.4	*N33° 35.37′ W111° 29.55′* Drop into next wash and turn south.

WP	Mile	Action
08	2.1 Reset	*N33° 34.87′ W111° 29.71′* Reach Cove #2. Enjoy, then turn around and go back up wash.
07	0.6	Return to Waypoint 07, only this time stay to right in another wash, continuing to head north.
	1.5	Turn right out of wash and cross over another ridge.
09	1.7	*N33° 35.94′ W111° 29.31′* Drop into another wash and head south.
10	3.2	*N33° 34.83′ W111° 29.44′* Reach Cove #3. Return trip: The easiest way is to go back the way you came. However, you can continue to head east to more coves and explore on your own. There are many confusing roads in the area, but if you know the big picture you can eventually find your way back to where you started. You'll find all kinds of surprises and unexpected obstacles, so be ready for anything.

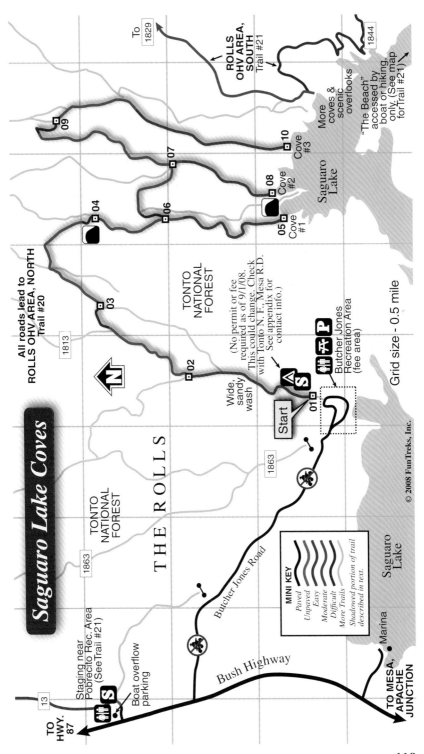

Saguaro Lake Coves

All roads lead to
ROLLS OHV AREA, NORTH
Trail #20

To 1829

ROLLS OHV AREA,
SOUTH
Trail #21

1844

More
coves &
scenic
overlooks

"The Beach"
accessed by
boat or hiking,
only. (See map
for Trail #21)

09

10

Cove
#3

07

08

Cove
#2

04

06

Saguaro Lake

05

Cove
#1

TONTO
NATIONAL
FOREST

03

1813

N

02

Wide,
sandy,
wash

(No permit or fee
required as of 9/1/08.
This could change. Check
with Tonto N. F. Mesa R.D.
See appendix for
contact info.)

Start

P

Butcher Jones
Recreation Area
(fee area)

Grid size - 0.5 mile

© 2008 FunTreks, Inc.

01

1863

TONTO
NATIONAL
FOREST

T H E   R O L L S

1863

Butcher Jones Road

MINI KEY

Paved
Unpaved
Easy
Moderate
Difficult
More Trails
Shadowed portion of trail
described in text.

Saguaro Lake

Marina

Staging near
Pobrecito Rec. Area
(See Trail #21)

13

Boat overflow
parking

Bush Highway

TO
HWY.
87

TO MESA,
APACHE
JUNCTION

119

View from F.S. 143 looking west near top.

F.S. 422 winds its way north.

Looking east from 422A at Roosevelt Lake.

Optional 422A is difficult.

Campspot at end of 422A. Hohokam Indian site?

Four Peaks

23

Getting There: From east side of Phoenix, take Highway 87 north. Just before mile marker 204, turn right on Four Peaks Road, F.S. 143. Drive east 0.7 miles to parking lot with vault toilet on right.

Staging/Camping: On weekends, main parking lot fills up quickly. It is very congested and people squeeze in anywhere they can fit. More parking and camping is available if you continue several miles east on F.S. 143. The staging area for this trail is the same as Rolls OHV Area, North, Trail #20. In fact, the entire Rolls OHV Area, including Trails #21 and #22, can be accessed from this point.

Difficulty: The main route described here is easy all the way; however, don't get complacent. Curves tighten as you climb. There are dangerous places where too much speed can send you flying off the road. Watch for fast-moving oncoming traffic and slow down for blind curves. The optional side trip down 422A is very steep with deep, tippy ruts. Parts of the trail, near the bottom, are partially washed out.

Highlights: Gorgeous high mountain views on a clear day. Although the road is wide, it is great fun to ride. Optional difficult side trip on 422A leads to a circle of giant boulders, a great camping spot. Numerous Indian grinding holes in the rock are an indication that this was probably an historic Hohokam Indian site. To extend trip on easy terrain, consider riding down the east side on El Oso Road. It continues an additional 9 miles to Hwy. 188. Make sure you have plenty of gas.

Time & Distance: We turned around at 23.6 miles; however, the road continues farther. Allow 4 to 5 hours for the 47-mile round trip and another hour for optional 422A.

Trail Description: You'll follow a wide gravel road as it climbs gently across Sonoran desert. Gradually, as you approach the peaks, the road begins to narrow and climbs more steeply. The best views occur after about 15 miles, before you reach the top. After Waypoint 04, you'll head north following a high scenic ridge.

Services: Vault toilet at staging area. No other facilities along the route. Bring plenty of gas and water. Return to outskirts of Phoenix for all services.

Directions: *(Shadowed portion of trail is described here.)*

WP	Mile	Action
01	0.0	*N33° 40.18′ W111° 29.73′* Head east on F.S. Road 143 from parking lot with toilet.
	1.4	Stay left on main road. (F.S. 401 goes right.)
02	2.7	*N33° 40.90′ W111° 28.02′* Stay right on main road. (F.S. 11 goes left.)
	9.7	Good camp spot on left with shade.
03	10.1	*N33° 43.54′ W111° 24.14′* Make hard right up switchback on main road. (143A and Cline Hiking Trail go left.)
	14.2	Continue on main road. (Mud Springs Hiking Trail on right goes to Four Peaks Wilderness.)
04	17.1	*N33° 43.27′ W111° 20.25′* Continue straight on main road. (F.S. 648 joins on right. This leads to another hiking trail into wilderness.)
05	18.2	*N33° 43.82′ W111° 20.87′* Bear left on F.S.422 at intersection with El Oso Road. (Right goes downhill on easier road to Highway 188.)
06	20.1	*N33° 44.75′ W111° 22.21′* Continue straight on 422. (Note: 422A goes right here. This is a great side trip, but it is washed out, rutted and very difficult. It leads to a circle of giant boulders that makes a great camp spot. We saw many grinding holes in the boulders, indicating that this was probably a Hohokam Indian site.
	23.6	We turned around at F.S. 463, marked with cairn on right. (Off edge of map.) This is an adopted 4WD trail that connects to 422A. We did not ride 463, but understand it passes El Oso Mine. F.S. 422 continues a considerable distance.
01	47.2	Return to staging area.

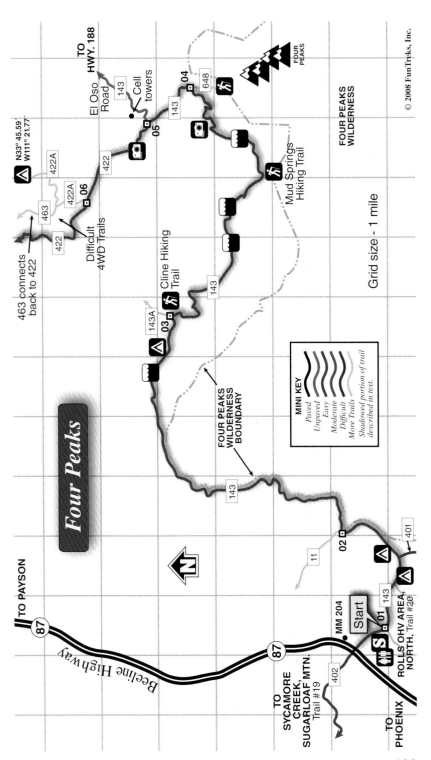

Four Peaks

TO PAYSON

Beeline Highway

87

TO SYCAMORE CREEK, SUGARLOAF MTN. Trail #19

TO PHOENIX

MM 204

Start

01

143

402

ROLLS OHV AREA, NORTH, Trail #20

401

02

11

N

FOUR PEAKS WILDERNESS BOUNDARY

143

143A

03

Cline Hiking Trail

Difficult 4WD Trails

06

422A

422A

463

422

463 connects back to 422

N33° 45.59' W111° 21.77'

422

422

05

143

El Oso Road

Cell towers

143

TO HWY. 188

04

648

Mud Springs Hiking Trail

FOUR PEAKS WILDERNESS

FOUR PEAKS

MINI KEY
Paved
Unpaved
Easy
Moderate
Difficult
More Trails
Shadowed portion of trail described in text.

Grid size - 1 mile

© 2008 FunTreks, Inc.

123

Staging area outside gate at Blue Point Entrance. Combination lock on gate.

Parts of canyon are easy.

Toughest spot at Wpt. 03 is quite steep and rutted.

Lots of rocks to negotiate.

Several banked curves on F.S. 1356.

View of Superstition Mountain approaching Waypoint 08.

124

Bulldog Canyon

24

Getting There: This description starts at the Blue Point Entrance on Bush Highway, located 1.7 miles east of Usery Pass Road. You may also enter at four other gates, shown on map.

Staging/Camping: Park and unload outside gate. Although camping is allowed along the trail, you seldom see anyone camping. Forest Service camping regulations apply.

Special Permit: A special permit is required for this trail. It's easy to obtain and is free. Each rider must have a permit and carry it with him at all times. To obtain a permit, contact the Mesa Ranger District of Tonto National Forest (see appendix for contact information). This is an environmentally sensitive area and is carefully monitored. *RIDE ON NUMBERED ROUTES ONLY.* An area north of Waypoint 05 looks like a terrain park; however, riding here is strictly forbidden. Violations could result in fines up to $5,000, or six months in jail.

Difficulty: First part of trail after Waypoint 02 winds back and forth across Bulldog Canyon, where it is steep and rocky in places. This portion may not be suitable for novice riders. With a few minor exceptions, the trail is relatively easy east of Waypoint 05.

Highlights: Conveniently located close to Phoenix, Mesa and Apache Junction. Great scenery and enough challenge to make it fun. The area is typically not as crowded as other riding areas, even though there is no limit to the number of permits issued.

Time & Distance: Round trip out and back is 26.6 miles. The best part of ride is between Waypoints 02 and 05. Entire round trip takes 4 to 5 hours.

Trail Description: Head south on easy road. After sandy wash, trail enters Bulldog Canyon, where it crosses back and forth across canyon under power lines. After Waypoint 05, trail heads east across hilly but easier terrain. To extend day, explore other numbered roads, including F.S. 3554, which goes west to Usery Pass Road.

Services: No facilities anywhere along the trail. Return to Phoenix, Mesa or Apache Junction for all services.

Directions: *(Shadowed portion of trail is described here.)*

WP	Mile	Action	WP	Mile	Action
01	0.0	N33° 33.06′ W111° 34.89′ From Blue Point Entrance, head south on F.S.10.	04	7.5	N33° 28.46′ W111° 32.33′ Bear left on larger road at T intersection.
02	2.3	N33° 31.33′ W111° 34.51′ Continue straight across wide, sandy wash. (F.S. 3554 goes right to Usery Entrance.)	05	8.1 Reset	N33° 28.29′ W111° 31.86′ Bear left on F.S. 1356. (Wolverine Entrance is straight ahead about 0.3 miles.)
	2.6	Cross wash under power lines.	06	0.9	N33° 29.02′ W111° 31.96′ Turn right.
	2.8	Stay right uphill.		2.5	Bear right before yellow mountain.
	5.5	Continue straight where road goes right.		3.2	Bear left at Y intersection.
03	5.6	N33° 29.34′ W111° 33.28′ Steep, rutted downhill section. Toughest part of trail.	07	3.2+	N33° 29.47′ W111° 30.04′ Just 200 ft. past last fork, continue straight on 1356 (see detail). Cross wash and climb hill.
	6.5	Stay left under power lines.		3.6	Bear left up steep hill. (You have several choices. First spot to turn is steepest.)
	6.8	Continue straight. (Lesser road crosses.)	08	5.2 Reset	N33° 28.75′ W111° 28.56′ F.S. 1356 ends at Cottonwood Entrance near Highway 88.
	7.1	Continue straight. (Road joins on right.)	01	13.3	Return to start.
	7.3	At top of hill, go through old gate.			

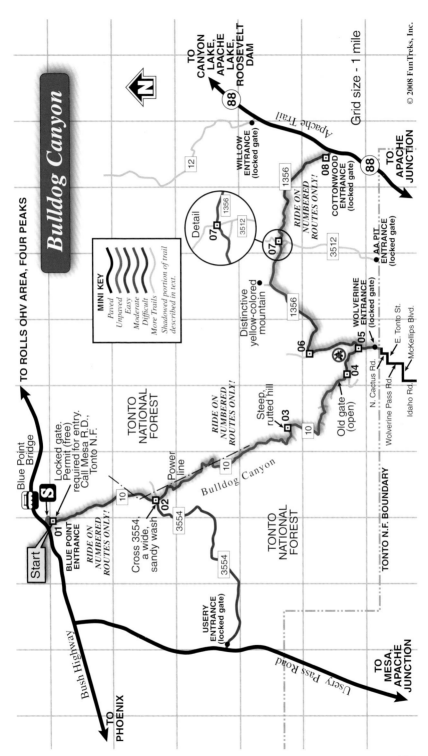

Bulldog Canyon

TO ROLLS OHV AREA, FOUR PEAKS

Grid size - 1 mile

© 2008 FunTreks, Inc.

N

MINI KEY
Paved
Unpaved
Easy
Moderate
Difficult
More Trails
Shadowed portion of trail described in text.

TO CANYON LAKE, APACHE LAKE, ROOSEVELT DAM

88

Apache Trail

WILLOW ENTRANCE (locked gate)

12

Detail

1356

3512

07

1356

07

RIDE ON NUMBERED ROUTES ONLY!

08

COTTONWOOD ENTRANCE (locked gate)

88

TO APACHE JUNCTION

3512

AA PIT ENTRANCE (locked gate)

Distinctive yellow-colored mountain

1356

WOLVERINE ENTRANCE (locked gate)

06

05

04

Old gate (open)

10

Steep, rutted hill

03

N. Cactus Rd.

E. Tonto St.

Wolverine Pass Rd.

McKellips Blvd.

Idaho Rd.

TONTO NATIONAL FOREST

RIDE ON NUMBERED ROUTES ONLY!

Bulldog Canyon

10

Power line

10

02

Cross 3554, a wide, sandy wash

3554

TONTO NATIONAL FOREST

3554

TONTO N.F. BOUNDARY

Blue Point Bridge

S

Start

Locked gate. Permit (free) required for entry. Call Mesa R.D., Tonto N.F.

01

BLUE POINT ENTRANCE

RIDE ON NUMBERED ROUTES ONLY!

10

Bush Highway

TO PHOENIX

USERY ENTRANCE (locked gate)

Usery Pass Road

TO MESA, APACHE JUNCTION

127

View just before entering wash on FR 172.

Switchbacks near middle of trail are fun to ride.   UTV friendly.

Wildflowers in June.   View from top of Montana Mountain looking south.

Beautiful view across valley heading north to Montana Mountain.

Montana Mountain

25

Getting There: From Phoenix, head east on Highway 60 past Apache Junction. Turn left on Queen Valley Road, marked with huge sign, 0.2 miles past mile marker 214. After 1.6 miles turn right on Hewitt Station Road, F.S. 357. We drove 0.7 miles to large staging area on left, but Hewitt Station Road has many places to stage.

Staging/Camping: Stage as described above. Several good camp spots along trail. **Alternate staging area:** From Florence Junction, head east on Highway 60. At 10.3 miles, turn left on Hewitt Station Road (there were no signs identifying this road). Cross cattle guard just before large parking area (Waypoint 07).

Difficulty: Easy to moderate. Hewitt Station Road is wide and well maintained. Watch for blind curves on some portions of F.S. 172. The trail is narrow and steep near Montana Mountain. Dangerous ice can be present in late fall. The area is remote and can get hot in summer; bring plenty of water. Hewitt Station Road can be busy with big trucks.

Highlights: Popular mountain ride with several great hiking trails. Very scenic trail, especially when viewed from high vantage points. Great loop with many sideroads.

Trail Description: Follow well-maintained road to first turn, then head north through beautiful canyon. Driver's choice as trail joins wash several times. After passing a windmill on your left, watch for oncoming traffic around blind curves. Road narrows and climbs rapidly as you approach Montana Mountain. Spectacular views as you continue along ridge with good camp spots on left side of trail. Turn around if icy. After descending switchbacks, you will continue through several small water crossings. Follow most traveled road south or explore the many optional side roads leading to the town of Superior. Head west on Hewitt Station Road towards start of trail to complete the loop.

Time & Distance: Trip as described totals 37 miles. Allow 4 to 5 hours. Explore other roads to extend day.

Services: Nothing on trail. Full services in Apache Junction and Superior.

Directions: *(Shadowed portion of trail is described here.)*

WP	Mile	Action
01	**0.0**	*N33° 16.74´ W111° 16.26´* From staging area, head east on F.S. 357.
02	**2.4** **Reset**	*N33° 18.05´ W111° 14.67´* Turn left crossing wash onto F.S. 172. Follow sign for Superstition Trailheads.
	3.7	Driver's choice at wash.
03	**9.2**	*N33° 23.91´ W111° 11.83´* Bear right on F.S. 172A as trail climbs. (Left on F.S. 172B goes to hiking trailhead.)
04	**12.8**	*N33° 25.05´ W111° 10.47´* Bear right on steep, narrow road. It is marked F.S. 650 farther up the hill. (Left goes to hiking trailhead.)
	14.2	Follow ridge. Scenic overlook on right.
	18.6	Descend switchbacks.
	20.8	Bear right where road joins from left. (Left goes to F.S. 342.)
05	**21.6**	*N33° 22.13´ W111° 07.04´* Continue straight on F.S. 650 as F.S. 342 joins from left.
	22.0	Continue straight crossing wash.
	22.6	Ignore lesser roads.
	23.4	Continue straight. (F.S. 2359 heads west to more trails.)
	26.1	Continue straight. (F.S. 1011 eventually leads back to Hewitt Station Road.)
06	**27.7**	*N33° 17.74´ W111° 08.90´* Bear right on Happy Camp Road, F.S. 8.
	28.8	Follow main road over train tracks where F.S. 293 joins main road from right.
07	**29.5**	*N33° 16.85´ W111° 10.28´* Turn right on Hewitt Station Road heading west. Alternate staging area is located here.
	33.1	Large shady camp spot on right.
02	**34.4**	End of loop. Staging area is another 2.4 miles heading west on Hewitt Station Road.

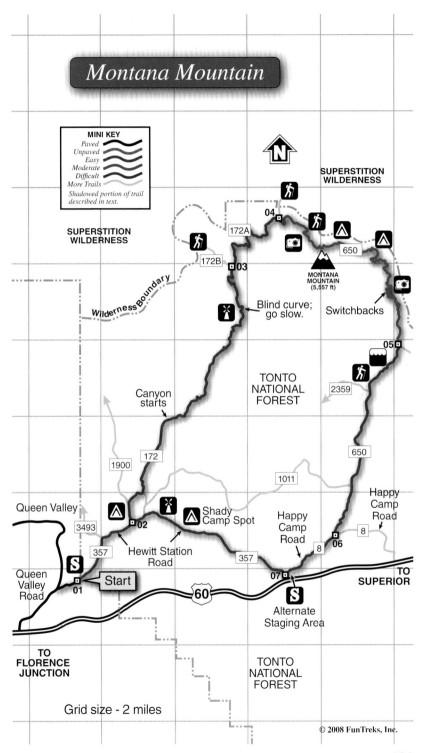

Montana Mountain

MINI KEY
Paved
Unpaved
Easy
Moderate
Difficult
More Trails
Shadowed portion of trail
described in text.

SUPERSTITION
WILDERNESS

SUPERSTITION
WILDERNESS

172A

172B

03

04

650

MONTANA
MOUNTAIN
(5,557 ft)

Switchbacks

Blind curve;
go slow.

05

2359

TONTO
NATIONAL
FOREST

Canyon
starts

172

1900

650

1011

Queen Valley

Happy
Camp
Road

3493

Shady
Camp Spot

02

Happy
Camp
Road

357

8

8

06

Hewitt Station
Road

357

TO
SUPERIOR

Queen
Valley
Road

01

Start

60

07

Alternate
Staging Area

TO
FLORENCE
JUNCTION

TONTO
NATIONAL
FOREST

Grid size - 2 miles

© 2008 FunTreks, Inc.

131

Staging area we selected on Price Road.

Small challenges in Box Canyon make ride fun.

No place to be in a flash flood.

Bypass route climbs along high ridge with great views.

Historic stage depot, south of Waypoint 04.

Bypass route avoids this big ledge.

Closure dates posted at entrances.

Box Canyon

Getting There: **To ride trail north:** From Florence, head north on Hwy. 79 about 2 miles and turn right on Price Road by the railroad tracks. Follow Price Road east, crossing back and forth across railroad tracks. We selected a staging area on the left at 10.9 miles, but more places were available just ahead. **To ride trail south:** Take Highway 60 east from Phoenix and continue about 16 miles past Apache Junction. Continue east past large sign for Queen Valley to Mineral Mountain Road and turn right before mile marker 216. Staging area is just ahead on right.

Staging/Camping: Stage as described above. Camping is available at various entry points (see map). We like camping in the 2-mile section after Waypoint 01. *Important: A state land permit is required to ride in this area.* In addition, this is a military training area and is closed several weeks each year. Dates are posted at various entry points. DO NOT ENTER IF RED FLAGS ARE FLYING ON FLAGPOLES.

Difficulty: Easy to moderate. This trail description bypasses a difficult obstacle between Waypoints 04 and 05. Do not ride this trail if thunderstorms are expected. Narrow Box Canyon is susceptible to high-water flash floods and can be very dangerous during heavy rain storms. Many roads branch off, making route-finding confusing if you don't follow directions carefully.

Highlights: Great fun through Box Canyon and over the bypass route, which follows a narrow, scenic high ridge. Stop and inspect an historic stage depot (see photo to left). The route described here bisects one of Arizona's most popular 4-wheeling areas and connects to well-known trails like Woodpecker Mine, Coke Ovens and Martinez Canyon. (See trails #27, #28 and #29 in this book.)

Time & Distance: One-way trip, decribed here, measures 16.5 miles. Allow 4 to 5 hours for round trip. Box Canyon, by itself, can be ridden both ways in about an hour.

Trail Description: The best part of this ride is the 7-mile stretch through Box Canyon and over the bypass. The balance of trip is intended primarily to describe how to enter the area from the north. Jeepers love the regular route between Waypoints 04 and 05 because of the giant ledge. ATVs can do it, but it's tough. Mineral Mountain Road is uneventful. Cottonwood Canyon Road has many camping places.

Services: Nothing along trail. Full services in Florence and Apache Junction. Gas and food along Highway 60, west of Florence Junction.

Directions: *(Shadowed portion of trail is described here.)*

WP	Mile	Action
01	0.0	*TO RIDE TRAIL NORTH* *N 33° 06.25´ W111° 13.53´* Head north from staging.
02	2.6	*N33° 07.85´ W111° 12.32´* Enter mouth of Box Canyon.
	4.0	Bear right uphill out of wash.
03	4.3	*N33° 08.98´ W111° 12.08´* Bear left in wash at yellow sign with arrow. (Trails #28 and #29 to right.)
04	5.9	*N33° 10.10´ W111° 12.08´* Bear right in sandy wash to start bypass. (Left has major obstacle.)
	7.0	Hard left up steep hill out of wash. Then stay left at 7.7 and 8.3 miles.
05	9.5	*N33° 11.83´ W111° 13.02´* Bear right and cross wash, then turn left on other side (see map detail).
	9.8	Continue straight (Woodpecker entrance on right.)
	9.9	Bear right uphill out of wash.
06	10.2	*N33° 12.16´ W111° 13.48´* Continue straight on Mineral Mtn. Road. (Left is Cottonwood Canyon Rd.)
	12.0	Bear right at Y. (Reymert Road goes left.)
07	16.5	*N33° 15.72´ W111° 16.53´* Alternate starting point.
07	0.0	*TO RIDE TRAIL SOUTH* Head south from alternate start on Mineral Mtn. Road.
	4.4	Continue straight. (Reymert Road joins on right.)
	4.7	Bear right. (Reymert Road departs to left.)
06	6.3	Continue straight. (Cottonwood Canyon Road is right.)
	6.4	Drop downhill and turn left in wide sandy wash.
	6.6	Continue straight. (Woodpecker entrance on left.)
05	7.1	Bear right, dip down and cross sandy wash. On other side, bear left to take easier bypass route (see detail).
	8.1	Stay right along high ridge. Then right again at 8.7.
	9.4	Descend steep hill, then turn right in sandy wash.
04	10.6	Continue straight. (Regular route joins on right.)
03	12.2	Continue straight at yellow sign through Box Canyon. (Martinez Canyon, #28, and Coke Ovens, #29, go left.)
02	14.0	Exit of Box Canyon. Wash leads to Price Road.
01	16.5	Staging area at southern entrance. Highway 79 is another 10.9 miles heading west on Price Road.

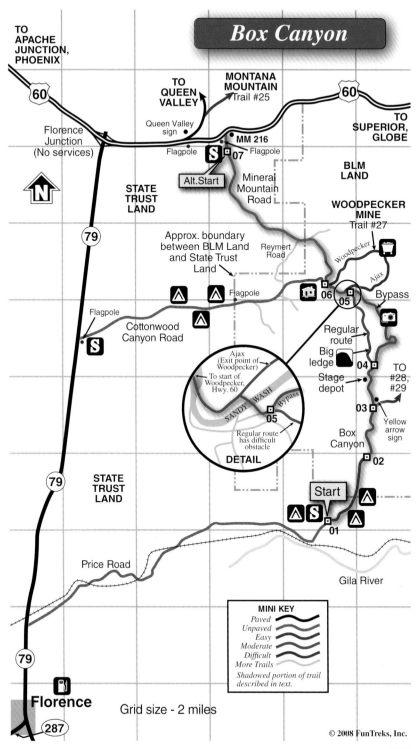

Box Canyon

TO APACHE JUNCTION, PHOENIX

60

TO SUPERIOR, GLOBE

60

TO QUEEN VALLEY

MONTANA MOUNTAIN Trail #25

Queen Valley sign

Florence Junction (No services)

Flagpole

MM 216

Flagpole

S 07

Alt.Start

Mineral Mountain Road

BLM LAND

STATE TRUST LAND

79

Approx. boundary between BLM Land and State Trust Land

Reymert Road

WOODPECKER MINE Trail #27

Woodpecker

Ajax

Bypass

06

05

Flagpole

Regular route

Flagpole

Cottonwood Canyon Road

S

Ajax (Exit point of Woodpecker)

To start of Woodpecker, Hwy. 60

Big ledge

04

TO #28, #29

Stage depot

03

Yellow arrow sign

SANDY WASH

Bypass

05

Regular route has difficult obstacle

Box Canyon

DETAIL

02

STATE TRUST LAND

Start

01

Price Road

Gila River

MINI KEY
Paved
Unpaved
Easy
Moderate
Difficult
More Trails
Shadowed portion of trail described in text.

79

Florence

287

Grid size - 2 miles

© 2008 FunTreks, Inc.

135

Entrance to Woodpecker is wide and harmless looking.

Deep notch on left is the Firehole. ATVs can bypass on the right.

This photo clearly shows why trail is not for novice riders.

Trail passes next to Woodpecker Mine.

Open range land; watch for cattle.

Woodpecker, Ajax Loop

Getting There: Take Highway 60 east from Phoenix and continue about 16 miles past Apache Junction. Continue east past large sign for Queen Valley to Mineral Mountain Road and turn right before mile marker 216. Check flagpole to make sure no red flag is flying and proceed short distance to staging area on right. Set odometer on ATV to zero and continue south on Mineral Mountain Road. Continue straight at 4.4 miles, where Reymert Road joins on right, then bear right at 4.7. Continue straight at 6.3 miles, where Cottonwood Canyon Road goes right. Drop downhill and swing left in wide, sandy wash. Entrance to Woodpecker is on left at 6.6 miles.

   You can also reach start of Woodpecker from the west side, off Highway 79 via Cottonwood Canyon Road, or from the south through Box Canyon. See map and directions for Box Canyon, Trail #26.

Staging/Camping: Stage as described above. Camp along Mineral Mountain Road, Cottonwood Canyon Road or on Price Road as described in Trail #26. ***Important: A state land permit is required to ride in this area.*** In addition, this is a military training area and is closed several weeks each year. Dates are posted at various entry points. DO NOT ENTER IF RED FLAGS ARE FLYING ON FLAGPOLES.

Difficulty: Requires climbing over and squeezing between large boulders. Tip-overs possible. For advanced riders only. *UTVs can go up Ajax, but should stay off Woodpecker.*

Highlights: Not a scenic trail. The only reason to ride here is to challenge yourself. A tougher trail for Jeeps than ATVs.

Time & Distance: Entire loop, returning to start, is just 5.6 miles. Allow 2 to 4 hours depending on riding skills.

Trail Description: Entrance to Woodpecker is wide, but trail quickly narrows. The first Jeep obstacle, called the Firehole, is impossible for ATVs, but has a bypass on the right. Devil's Back is tippy, but relatively easy. The V-Notch is narrow for Jeeps, but wide enough for ATVs. Follow a twisty road over a ridge between Woodpecker and Ajax, then descend easier Ajax back to start.

Services: No services of any kind after you leave pavement. Full services in Apache Junction and Florence. Highway 60 has a shopping center and gas station near mile marker 202.

Directions: *(Shadowed portion of trail is described here.)*

WP	Mile	Action
01	0.0	*N33° 12.03´ W111° 13.41´* Leave main wash and head north in Woodpecker.
	0.4	Stay to right side of wash to go around the Firehole, an extreme Jeep obstacle.
	0.9	Approach Devil's Back obstacle. We found going through on left side easier.
	1.7	Continue straight. Don't go right.
	1.8	Pass through the V-Notch. (This obstacle is much harder for Jeeps.)
02	2.2	*N33° 12.86´ W111° 12.20´* Turn hard right uphill out of wash. (Straight is Upper Woodpecker, called "Highway to Hell.")
	2.3	Stay right to get around rocky ledge.
	2.5	Bear right at T intersection.
03	2.6	*N33° 12.85´ W111° 11.85´* Stay left past Woodpecker Mine.
	3.0	Washed-out road climbs and descends. Large ruts are tippy in places.

WP	Mile	Action
04	3.1	*N33° 12.57´ W111° 11.67´* Bear right. (Road that joins on left ends at mine.)
05	3.4	*N33° 12.37´ W111° 11.58´* Turn hard right towards rusty water tank to start Ajax. Road weaves back and forth across rocky wash. For more challenge, you can ride in wash.
06	4.0	*N33° 12.03´ W111° 11.99´* Continue straight. Road joins on left.
	4.6	Pass through cattle watering hole with windmill.
07	5.2	*N33° 11.85´ W111° 13.06´* Continue straight, then follow wash to right to return to start of Woodpecker. (Left across wash leads to Box Canyon, Trail #26, via choice of two different routes shown on map.)
01	5.6	Return to start of Woodpecker.

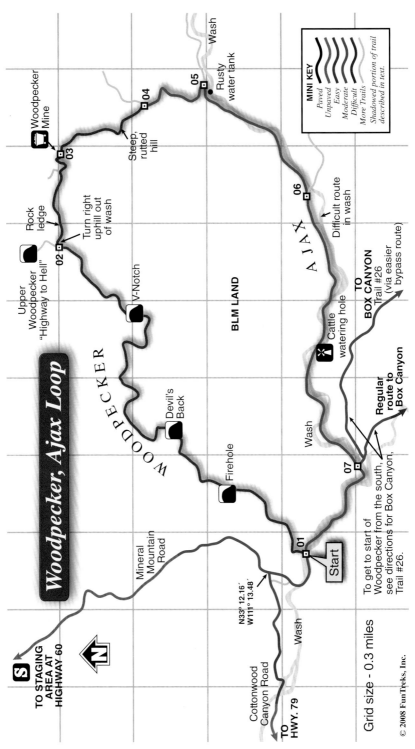

Woodpecker, Ajax Loop

MINI KEY

Paved
Unpaved
Easy
Moderate
Difficult
More Trails
Shadowed portion of trail described in text.

Wash

05 Rusty water tank

04

Steep, rutted hill

Woodpecker Mine

03

Rock ledge

Turn right uphill out of wash

Upper Woodpecker "Highway to Hell"

02

V-Notch

06

Difficult route in wash

A J A X

BLM LAND

Cattle watering hole

TO BOX CANYON Trail #26 (via easier bypass route)

Devil's Back

W O O D P E C K E R

Wash

Regular route to Box Canyon

Firehole

07

Mineral Mountain Road

01

Start

N33° 12.16′ W111° 13.48′

To get to start of Woodpecker from the south, see directions for Box Canyon, Trail #26.

N

Cottonwood Canyon Road

Wash

TO HWY. 79

TO STAGING AREA AT HIGHWAY 60

Grid size - 0.3 miles

© 2008 FunTreks, Inc.

View below Waypoint 02.

Climbing down the "Luge."

Trail (foreground) passes below Martinez Mill.

Believe it or not, this is a bypass.

Steep shelf road climbs to Waypoint 07.

Martinez Cabin has collapsed. Keep out.

Martinez Canyon ◆28◆

Getting There: The start of this trail can be reached from three different directions. Look at the map for Box Canyon, Trail #26, for an overview. The Price Road entrance is described below because it offers good camping, is the most direct route, and is the most fun. To enter via Price Road, head north from Florence about 2 miles on Highway 79 and turn right before the railroad tracks. Head east, weaving back and forth across the tracks. After about 10 miles, the road turns north towards Box Canyon. Unload and/or camp anywhere within the next three miles and proceed to entrance to Box Canyon. Continue another 1.7 miles through Box Canyon to a large 3-way intersection in a wide, sandy wash. Look for a dented yellow sign with a black arrow. The trail is uphill to the right. Avoid steep climbs hard right.

Staging/Camping: Stage or camp as described above. ***Important: A state land permit is required to ride in this area.*** In addition, this is a military training area and is closed several weeks each year. Dates are posted on signs at various entry points. DO NOT ENTER IF RED FLAGS ARE FLYING ON FLAGPOLES.

Difficulty: The ride to Martinez Cabin is rocky and steep in a few places, but mostly moderate. A narrow section before the cabin is borderline difficult. After the cabin, it becomes extremely rocky with a very difficult boulder field. Most people stop here and walk the short distance to Martinez Mill. Riding beyond the mill is extremely difficult and dangerous. We were able to ride another mile past the mill, but were finally stopped by large ledges with no place to attach a winch line. We hiked to the "Luge," an obstacle not recommended for ATVs. To see the Luge without hiking, ride up from the bottom from Wpt. 05. *Not recommended for UTVs beyond Martinez Cabin.*

Highlights: This trail has it all: incredible scenery, historic mine buildings, and enough challenge for anyone.

Time & Distance: After you reach the start of trail, the 3.7-mile, one-way trip to Martinez Cabin takes less than an hour. The mill is 0.5 miles past the cabin. Time in Martinez Canyon varies depending on skill level.

Trail Description: Head east over a scenic ridge and descend to historic Martinez Cabin. Ride as far as skill level allows to Martinez Mill, then hike, if necessary. Advanced riders only beyond the mill.

Services: No services of any kind after you leave pavement. Full services in Apache Junction and Florence.

Directions: *(Shadowed portion of trail is described here.)*

WP	Mile	Action
01	0.0	*N33° 08.98′ W111° 12.08′* Head northeast, climbing out of sandy wash. As you climb, stay left on main road. Roads to right eventually come back to main trail.
	0.3	Stay right uphill on main road, passing a water tank with collapsing windmill.
02	0.8	*N33° 09.23′ W111° 11.44′* Cattle guard marks scenic high point. Continue straight down other side.
	1.2	Bear right. (Lesser wash goes left.) Climb and descend through scenic area.
03	2.1	*N33° 09.19′ W111° 10.61′* Cross wash at bottom and bear left. (Trail 29 goes right.)
	2.4	Trail narrows and gets rockier.
	3.6	Hidden in brush on right is large, shallow cave. (This was once a cantina and bordello for mine workers. Watch for spiders.)
04	3.7	*N33° 09.86′ W111° 09.67′* Martinez Cabin. Good lunch spot with shade.
05	3.8	*N33° 09.87′ W111° 09.64′* Bear right to reach Martinez Mill. (Left climbs to base of the "Luge.")
	4.0	Trail gets very difficult with large boulders. We took bypass to right (see photo).
06	4.2	*N33° 10.03′ W111° 09.33′* Arrive at Martinez Mill. If you want to continue, stay in the wash that goes through the mill. The road uphill to the right dead ends. The main trail climbs in and out of the wash, then begins a steep climb on a narrow, dangerous shelf road to Silver Bell Mine. Road may be washed out in places.
07	5.3	*N33° 10.60′ W111° 09.52′* After passing the Silver Bell Mine, you'll reach a high point, which is followed by a short but very steep descent. At this point we elected to park our ATVs and walk another half mile to the "Luge."

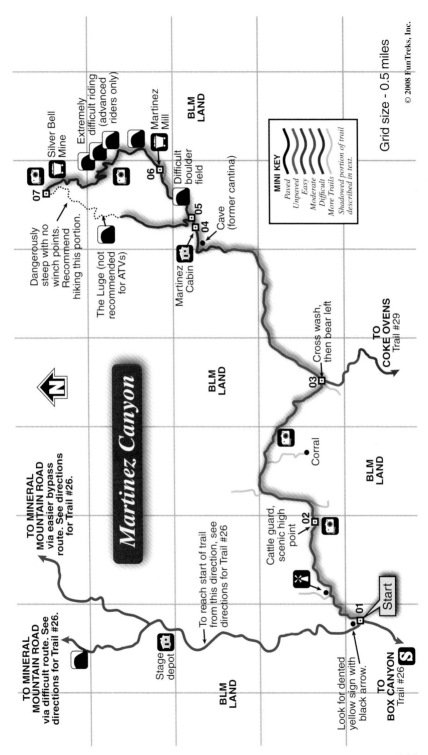

Martinez Canyon

Grid size - 0.5 miles

© 2008 FunTreks, Inc.

MINI KEY
Paved
Unpaved
Easy
Moderate
Difficult
More Trails
Shadowed portion of trail
described in text.

07

Silver Bell Mine

Extremely difficult riding (advanced riders only)

Martinez Mill

BLM LAND

06

Difficult boulder field

05

04

Cave (former cantina)

Martinez Cabin

Dangerously steep with no winch points. Recommend hiking this portion.

The Luge (not recommended for ATVs)

N

03

Cross wash, then bear left

TO COKE OVENS
Trail #29

Corral

BLM LAND

BLM LAND

02

Cattle guard, scenic high point

TO MINERAL MOUNTAIN ROAD via easier bypass route. See directions for Trail #26.

TO MINERAL MOUNTAIN ROAD via difficult route. See directions for Trail #26.

To reach start of trail from this direction, see directions for Trail #26

Stage depot

BLM LAND

01

Start

Look for dented yellow sign with black arrow.

TO BOX CANYON
Trail #26

S

Great scenery as trail climbs and descends series of ridges.

Careful tire placement needed in spots.

Cacti bloom in April.

Coke Ovens, five in all, remain in excellent condition.

Toughest obstacle is after the Coke Ovens.

Steep and rocky in places.

Coke Ovens

29

Getting There: The start of this trail can be reached from three different directions. Look at the map for Box Canyon, Trail #26, for an overview. The Price Road entrance is described below because it offers good camping, is the most direct route, and is the most fun. To enter via Price Road, head north from Florence about 2 miles on Highway 79 and turn right before the railroad tracks. Head east, weaving back and forth across the tracks. After about 10 miles, the road turns north towards Box Canyon. Unload and/or camp anywhere within the next three miles and proceed to entrance to Box Canyon. Continue another 1.7 miles through Box Canyon to a large 3-way intersection in a wide, sandy wash. Look for a dented yellow sign with a black arrow.

Staging/Camping: Stage or camp as described above. ***Important: A state land permit is required to ride in this area.*** In addition, this is a military training area and is closed several weeks each year. Dates are posted on signs at various entry points. DO NOT ENTER IF RED FLAGS ARE FLYING ON FLAGPOLES.

Difficulty: Most of trail is easy to moderate. A few steep, rocky sections after Waypoint 03 are borderline difficult. The most difficult spot is after the Coke Ovens. This spot can can be avoided by turning around at the Coke Ovens and returning the way you came.

Highlights: A fun ride to unusual historic structures. The ovens were used in the early 1900s to make coke, a clean-burning fuel used in blast furnaces to produce iron ore. Coke was made by baking a mixture of different kinds of coal at high temperature without contact with air.

Time & Distance: Round trip is 14 miles and takes 3 to 4 hours.

Trail Description: After an exciting trip through Box Canyon to start of trail, you'll begin climbing and descending a series of rocky ridges, many offering outstanding views. Intermittent challenges leave no time for boredom. Take time to inspect the remarkably intact Coke Ovens, but make sure to leave them exactly as you find them and please don't leave any trash behind. The two big ledges after the ovens should not be attempted by novice riders.

Services: No services of any kind after you leave pavement. Full services in Apache Junction and Florence.

Directions: *(Shadowed portion of trail is described here.)*

WP	Mile	Action
01	0.0	N33° 08.98´ W111° 12.08´ Head northeast, climbing out of sandy wash. As you climb, stay left on main road. Roads to right eventually come back to main trail.
	0.3	Stay right uphill on main road, passing a water tank with collapsing windmill.
02	0.8	N33° 09.23´ W111° 11.44´ Cattle guard marks scenic high point. Continue straight down other side.
	1.2	Bear right. (Lesser wash goes left.) Climb and descend through scenic area.
03	2.1 Reset	N33° 09.19´ W111° 10.61´ Cross wash at bottom and bear right. (Trail #28 goes left.)
	0.5	Climb up big step.
	0.9	High point with great views.
	1.6	Cross dry creek bed. (Difficult Jeep trail to left.)
	2.4	Long downhill stretch with big steps.
04	2.6	N33° 07.52´ W111° 10.25´ Stay left to start loop.
	3.2	Bear right.
05	4.1	N33° 06.91´ W111° 09.55´ Bear right.
	4.7	Bear left downhill.
	5.0	Make hard right through sandy area with roads going various directions. Weave your way uphill to Coke Ovens.
06	5.1	N33° 06.27´ W111° 09.89´ Arrive at Coke Ovens. You can turn around and go back the way you came to avoid a difficult spot OR circle around the back of the ovens and follow road uphill. Directions that follow continue around the loop.
	6.0	Two big ledges to climb, then trail swings left.
	7.0	Bear left.
04	7.2	Return to start of loop. Bear left to return the way you came.
01	11.9	Return to starting point. Left goes back to Price Road. Right goes to other entry points. See Trail #26 for details.

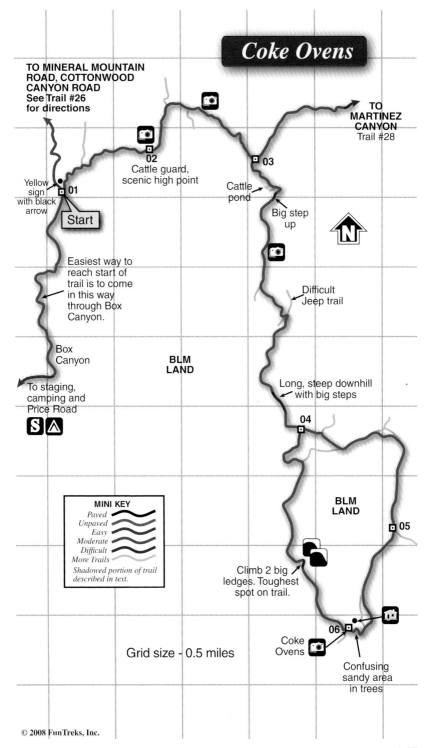

Coke Ovens

TO MINERAL MOUNTAIN
ROAD, COTTONWOOD
CANYON ROAD
See Trail #26
for directions

TO
MARTINEZ
CANYON
Trail #28

Yellow
sign
with black
arrow

🔲 01

Start

02
Cattle guard,
scenic high point

🔲 03

Cattle
pond

Big step
up

N

Easiest way to
reach start of
trail is to come
in this way
through Box
Canyon.

Difficult
Jeep trail

Box
Canyon

BLM
LAND

To staging,
camping and
Price Road

S A

Long, steep downhill
with big steps

04

MINI KEY
Paved
Unpaved
Easy
Moderate
Difficult
More Trails
*Shadowed portion of trail
described in text.*

BLM
LAND

05

Climb 2 big
ledges. Toughest
spot on trail.

Grid size - 0.5 miles

06

Coke
Ovens

Confusing
sandy area
in trees

Plenty of room to park at start of Battle Axe Road.

Fun obstacle as you enter a wash.

Very steep and rutted here.

Great views from high points along trail.

Gila River in late April.

We spotted this Gila Monster along trail.

Returning to start of loop.

Walnut Canyon

30

Getting There: From Phoenix, take Highway 60 east to Apache Junction, then continue another 28 miles to Superior. On east side of Superior, take Highway 177, Ray Road, south 9.5 miles. At top of hill, turn right onto Battle Axe Road.

Staging/Camping: You can park and unload at the beginning of Battle Axe Road or drive in a short distance. Battle Axe Road is usually in reasonably good condition, although it is not county maintained. Camping is permitted along Battle Axe Road, where BLM rules apply.

Difficulty: Moderate. A few small challenges in the washes. Toughest stretch is between Waypoints 05 and 06, where a long, steep downhill section is often deeply rutted and washed out, creating tippy situations that may be intimidating to novice riders. Much of trail follows low-lying sandy washes, in which flash floods are always possible. Keep an eye on the sky for potential heavy thunderstorms.

Highlights: Beautiful Sonoran desert framed with towering red buttes. A fun ride offering real adventure. Hike into White Canyon Wilderness north of the trail. A small part of this trail, at the south end along the Gila River, crosses state trust land, which, technically, requires a state trust land permit.

Time & Distance: Round trip, as described here, is almost 20 miles. Allow 4 to 5 hours. Extend day by exploring a network of side roads west of Waypoint 10. We were told by locals that you can reach the Coke Ovens from this trail; however, maps show this to be a long and complex trip. Don't try it unless you have someone with you who knows the way.

Trail Description: After a short stretch of easy road, you enter a narrow wash with small, fun obstacles. Exit this wash and begin a long climb to a scenic high ridge. First part of loop has a long, challenging descent to a wide wash, which heads due south towards the Gila River. You'll head west along the river across state trust land, then take another wash north. You turn out of this wash, at a point that's hard to find, and pass through a network of confusing roads. Fortunately, a natural wash takes you north on a distinct road back to where the loop began. You can see the Gila River by taking side trips south at Waypoint 07 or 08.

Services: Full services in Superior. Nothing along trail.

Directions: *(Shadowed portion of trail is described here.)*

WP	Mile	Action
01	0.0	*N33° 10.76´ W111° 02.37´* Head southwest on wide, easy Battle Axe Road.
02	1.3	*N33° 09.83´ W111° 02.98´* Turn right on lesser road. When road hits wash, bear left.
03	2.0	*N33° 09.68´ W111° 03.59´* Turn right on better road.
	3.0	Road continues in wash through trees. Small obstacles are fun.
04	3.6	*N33° 09.45´ W111° 04.85´* Bear right out of wash onto defined road and begin to climb.
	4.2	Bear left at Y. (Right dead ends at wilderness.)
	4.5	Cross wash, begin climb.
	5.1	Stay right downhill after switchbacks.
05	5.3	*N33° 09.01´ W111° 05.58´* Turn left to begin loop. Road climbs to views, then long, steep descent.
06	8.1	*N33° 07.99´ W111° 04.05´* After several small washes, turn right (due south) in large, sandy wash.
07	9.1	*N33° 07.20´ W111° 04.22´* Bear right into lesser wash and follow fence line west. If you miss this turn, you will end up at the river.
	9.5	Cross small wash and climb short, steep hill.
08	10.3	*N33° 06.98´ W111° 05.32´* Turn right in brushy wash that may not be obvious. (Left goes to river.) As you go north, wash becomes better defined, but splits various ways. Stay in wash.
09	11.6	*N33° 07.88´ W111° 05.13´* Turn left up steep bank out of wash onto defined road. Very easy to miss this turn. White arrow painted on rock is faint.
	11.8	Pass through barbed wire gate. Close it.
	12.1	Stay right, then right again as you climb.
10	12.4	*N33° 08.01´ W111° 05.63´* Hard left downhill. Then stay right to reach road in wash.
	13.4	Follow switchbacks uphill along shelf road.
05	14.1	Return to start of loop and continue straight, returning the way you came in.
01	19.4	Return to start.

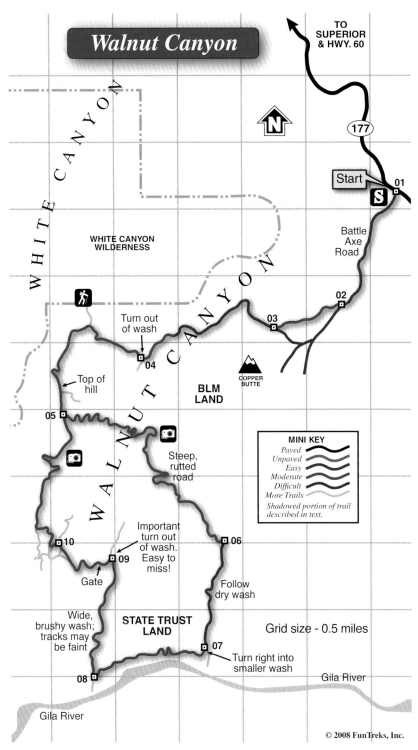

Walnut Canyon

TO
SUPERIOR
& HWY. 60

N

177

Start

S

01

Battle
Axe
Road

02

WHITE CANYON
WILDERNESS

Turn out
of wash

03

04

COPPER
BUTTE

BLM
LAND

Top of
hill

05

Steep,
rutted
road

MINI KEY
Paved
Unpaved
Easy
Moderate
Difficult
More Trails
Shadowed portion of trail
described in text.

Important
turn out
of wash.
Easy to
miss!

10

09

06

Gate

Follow
dry wash

Wide,
brushy wash;
tracks may
be faint

STATE TRUST
LAND

Grid size - 0.5 miles

07

Turn right into
smaller wash

08

Gila River

Gila River

© 2008 FunTreks, Inc.

151

View from top of 5,681-ft. Harquahala Mountain, Trail #1, easy.

Staging area for Sycamore Creek, Sugarloaf Mountain, Trail #19, moderate.

One of many coves at Saguaro Lake, Trails #21 and #22, difficult.

APPENDIX

Many great places to camp around Four Peaks, Trails #20 through #23.

References/Reading

Arizona Atlas & Gazetteer, by Delorme Mapping Company, Yarmouth, ME. Oversize 68-page map atlas of entire state of Arizona. (ISBN 978-0-89933-325-0, revised annually)

Arizona Ghost Towns and Mining Camps, Text by Philip Varney, Prepared by Book Division of Arizona Highways, Phoenix, AZ. Photos, stories and maps of Arizona's famous ghost towns. (1998)

Arizona Handbook, by Bill Weir, Avalon Travel Publishing, Chico, CA. Comprehensive recreation guide with photos and maps. (1999)

Arizona Place Names, by Will C. Barnes, University of Arizona Press, Tucson, AZ. Alphabetical reference of lesser-known places in Arizona. (1997)

ATV Riding, published by Tread Lightly!®, Ogden, UT. Small 24-page booklet with ATV riding tips and minimum impact recommendations. (2005)

(The) Back Roads, Prepared by Book Division of Arizona Highways, Phoenix, AZ. Forty full-color backroad tours for the whole family. (2007)

Back Roads and Beyond, by Pete Cowgill, Broken Toe Press, Tucson, AZ. Guide to southern Arizona truck and foot routes. (1997)

Crown King and the Southern Bradshaws: A Complete History, by Bruce M. Wilson, Crown King Press, Chandler, AZ. Photo illustrated history of Crown King mining days. (Published in 1992, may be out of print.)

Desert Survival Handbook, by Charles A. Lehman, Primer Publishers, Phoenix, AZ. A basic guide to desert survival. (1998)

GPS Made Easy, by Lawrence Letham, published by The Mountaineers Books, Seattle, WA. Handbook covers the basics of GPS. (ISBN 0898868238, 2003)

Roadside History of Arizona 2nd Edition, by Marshall Trimble, Mountain Press Publishing Company, Missoula. History of places along Arizona highways. (2004)

Scenic Driving Arizona 2nd Edition, by Stewart M. Green, Falcon Publishing, Inc., Helena, MT. Thirty scenic, mostly-paved drives. Includes maps and photos. (2003)

Contact Information

Bureau of Land Management
Web site: www.blm.gov/az

Arizona State Office
One North Central Avenue
Suite 800
Phoenix, AZ 85004-4427
(602) 417-9200

Explore Arizona Outdoor Information Center
One North Central Avenue
Suite 120
Phoenix, AZ 85004
(602) 417-9300
www.explorearizona.org

Phoenix District Hassayampa Field Office
21605 North 7th Avenue
Phoenix, AZ 85027-2929
(623) 580-5500

Chambers of Commerce

Apache Junction- (480) 982-3141
Black Canyon City-(623) 374-9797
Carefree-Cave Ck (480) 488-3381
Chandler (480) 963-4571
Florence- (520) 868-9433
Glendale- (623) 937-4754
Mayer- (928) 632-4355
Mesa- (480) 969-1307
Peoria- (623) 979-3601
Phoenix- (602) 495-2195
Prescott- (928) 445-2000
Scottsdale- (480) 355-2700
Superior- (520) 689-0200
Tempe- (480) 967-7891
Wickenberg- (800) 942-5242

Forest Service
Web site: www.fs.fed.us

Prescott N.F./ Supervisors Office
344 South Cortez Street
Prescott, AZ 86303
(928) 443-8000

Prescott N.F./ Bradshaw Ranger District
344 South Cortez Street
Prescott, AZ 86303
(928) 443-8000

Prescott Fire Center
2400 Melville Road
Prescott, AZ 86301
(928) 777-5610

Tonto N.F./ Supervisors Office
2324 East McDowell Road
Phoenix, AZ 85006
(602) 225-5200

Tonto N.F./ Cave Creek Ranger District
40202 North Cave Creek Road
Scottsdale, AZ 85262
(480) 595-3300

Tonto N.F./ Globe Ranger District
7680 South Six Shooter Canyon Rd.
Globe, AZ 85501
(928) 402-6200

Tonto N.F./ Mesa Ranger District
5140 E. Ingram Street
Mesa, AZ 85205
(480) 610-3300

Tonto N.F./ Payson Ranger District
1009 East Highway 260
Payson, AZ 85541
(928) 474-7900

Tonto N.F./ Tonto Basin Ranger District
State Hwy. 188
Roosevelt, AZ 85545
(928) 467-3200

GPS Sources

DeLorme Mapping
P. O. Box 298
Yarmouth, ME 04096
(800) 561-5105
www.delorme.com

Garmin International
1200 E. 151st Street
Olathe, KS 66062
(800) 800-1020
www.garmin.com

GPS NOW
www.GPSNOW.com

Lowrance Electronics, Inc.
12000 E. Skelly Drive
Tulsa, OK 74128
(800) 324-1356
www.lowrance.com

Magellan Corporation
(909) 394-5000
www.magellangps.com

National Geographic Maps
P.O. Box 4357
Evergreen, CO 80437
(800) 962-1643
www.nationalgeographic.com/maps

Important Agencies

Agua Fria National Monument
BLM Hassayampa Field Office
21605 North 7th Avenue
Phoenix, AZ 85027-2929
(623) 580-5500
www.blm.gov

Arizona Department of Environmental Quality
1110 W. Washington Street
Phoenix, AZ 85007
(602) 771-2300
www.azdeq.gov
(click on "Text/SMS Alerts" to sign up for OHV restriction dates)

Arizona Department of Transportation
Motor Vehicle Division
P.O. Box 2100
Phoenix, AZ 85001-2100
(602) 255-0072
www.azdot.gov

Arizona Game and Fish Department, Main Office
5000 W. Carefree Highway
Phoenix, AZ 85086-5000
(602) 942-3000
www.azgfd.gov

Arizona Office of Tourism
1110 W. Washington Street
Suite 155
Phoenix, AZ 85007
(602) 364-3700
www.azot.gov

Arizona State Land Department (Permits)
1616 West Adams
Phoenix, AZ 85007
(602) 542-4631
Web site: www.land.state.az.us

Arizona State Parks
1300 W. Washington Street
Phoenix, AZ 85007
(602) 542-4174
www.azstateparks. com

Lake Pleasant Regional Park
41835 N. Castle Hot Springs Road
Morristown, AZ 85342
(928) 501-1710
www.maricopa.gov/parks/
lake_pleasant

Other Helpful Contacts:

Arizona ATV Clubs
www.atvsource.com/clubs/state/
arizona.htm

Arizona ATV Riders
www.azatvriders.org

Arizona Site Stewards
To report vandalism
Call 1 (800) VANDALS

**Arizona State Association of
4-Wheel Drive Clubs**
P.O. Box 23904
Tempe, AZ 85285
(602) 258-4294
Web site: www.asa4wdc.org

**ATVA
All-Terrain Vehicle Association**
13515 Yarmouth Drive
Pickerington, OH 43147
(866) 288-2564
www.atvaonline.com

BlueRibbon Coalition
4555 Burley Drive Ste. A
Pocatello, ID 83202-1921
(800) 258-3742
www.sharetrails.org

Crown King General Store
(928) 632-7911

GPS File Conversion
(Free file conversion for most GPS
file formats)
www.gpsbabel.org

Lake and River Levels
www.azgfd.gov
(click on Hunting & Fishing, then
Lake/River Levels.

**National Forest Service
Nationwide Camping Reservations**
(877) 444-6777
www.recreation.gov

Ram Mounts
(mounts for GPS units)
(206) 763-8361
www.ram-mount.com

Tread Lightly
298 24th Street, Suite 325
Ogden, UT 84401
(800) 966-9900
Web site: www.treadlightly.org

Wag Bags® "Toilet in a Bag"
www.thepett.com

Wide World of Maps, Inc.
2626 West Indian School Road
Phoenix, AZ 85017-4397
(602) 279-2323

About the Authors

Charles (Chuck) Wells lives in Monument, CO, where he owns and manages *FunTreks Guidebooks*, a small publishing company he started in 1998. He graduated from Ohio State University in 1969 with a degree in graphic design and moved to Colorado in 1980, where he worked 18 years in the printing business. He is married with two grown children and four grandchildren. He bought a 4-wheel-drive SUV in 1994 and began exploring Colorado's backcountry. Later, he joined a 4-wheel-drive club and got more serious about four wheeling. In 1998, he wrote his first guidebook, *Guide to Colorado Backroads & 4-Wheel Drive Trails*, which was an immediate success. This enabled him to leave his regular job and write fulltime. To date, he has written eight SUV/Jeeping guidebooks (two are in second editions) and four ATV books. He first visited Arizona in 2000 while driving trails for his fourth book, *Guide to Arizona Backroads & 4-Wheel Drive Trails*.

Matt (PT) Peterson joined FunTreks in February of 2008. He graduated from Bethel College in Indiana with a degree in graphic design and came to Colorado in 2002. He is married and lives in Colorado Springs. Matt, a graphic designer and computer technician before joining FunTreks, works with Chuck writing books and provides much-needed computer and online support. Along with driving offroad, he enjoys maintaining and modifying FunTreks vehicles. Matt loves riding ATVs and being outdoors. He and Chuck rode all the trails in this book in April and May of 2008.

Authors Chuck Wells and Matt Peterson on Trail #3, near Morristown, AZ.

Order Form

Order 4 ways: (We accept Visa, Mastercard, Discover, American Express)
1. Call toll-free **1-877-222-7623**
2. Online at www.funtreks.com (secure site)
3. By Mail: Send this completed order form to:
   FunTreks, Inc, P. O. Box 3127, Monument, CO 80132
4. Fax this completed order form to 719-277-7411.

Please send me the following book(s): (I understand that, if I am not completely satisfied, I may return the book(s) for a full refund, no questions asked.)

Qty.

ATV Trails Guide Arizona Phoenix Region
    ISBN 978-1-934838-02-0, 160 pages, Price $19.95   _____

ATV Trails Guide Colorado Taylor Park, Crested Butte
    ISBN 978-1-934838-01-3, 160 pages, Price $19.95   _____

ATV Trails Guide Colorado Central Mountains
    ISBN 978-0-9664976-9-4, 168 pages, Price $19.95   _____

ATV Trails Guide Moab, UT
    ISBN 978-0-9664976-7-0, 160 pages, Price $18.95   _____

Guide to Arizona Backroads & 4-Wheel Drive Trails
    ISBN 978-0-9664976-3-2, 286 pages, Price $24.95   _____

Guide to Colorado Backroads & 4-Wheel Drive Trails (2nd Edition)
    ISBN 978-0-9664976-6-3, 286 pages, Price $24.95   _____

Guide to Northern Colorado Backroads & 4-Wheel Drive Trails
    ISBN 978-0-9664976-8-7, 192 pages, Price $19.95   _____

Guide to Moab, UT Backroads & 4-Wheel Drive Trails (2nd Edition)
    ISBN 978-1-934838-00-6, 224 pages, Price $27.95   _____

Guide to Southern California Backroads & 4-Wheel Drive Trails
    ISBN 978-0-9664976-4-9, 286 pages, Price $24.95   _____

Guide to Northern California Backroads & 4-Wheel Drive Trails
    ISBN 978-0-9664976-5-6, 286 pages, Price $24.95   _____

Name: (please print)_____

Address:_____

City:_____ State:____ Zip:_____

Telephone: (_____) _____-_____

Sales Tax: Colorado residents add 2.9%. (Subject to change without notice.)

Shipping: $5.00 for 1 or 2 books. Free shipping for 3 or more books.

Payment Method: Check one:

_____ Check

_____ Visa

_____ Mastercard   Card number:_____

_____ Discover   Expiration Date:_____

_____ American Express   Name on card:_____

FunTreks complete line of books

30 trails, 160 pgs, $19.95
ISBN 978-1-934838-02-0

75 trails, 286 pgs, $24.95
ISBN 978-0-9664976-3-2

55 trails, 224 pgs, $27.95
ISBN 978-1-934838-00-6

30 trails, 160 pgs, $19.95
ISBN 978-1-934838-01-3

75 trails, 286 pgs, $24.95
ISBN 978-0-9664976-6-3

45 trails, 192 pgs, $19.95
ISBN 978-0-9664976-8-7

32 trails, 168 pgs, $19.95
ISBN 978-0-9664976-9-4

75 trails, 286 pgs, $24.95
ISBN 978-0-9664976-5-6

75 trails, 286 pgs, $24.95
ISBN 978-0-9664976-4-9

30 trails, 160 pgs, $18.95
ISBN 978-0-9664976-7-0

TRAIL
Go to
www.funtreks.com
UPDATES